Eyewitness

DANCE

Tibetan
dance mask

Bharata
natyam
dancer

Ballet tutu

Nigerian
dance staff

Headdress for
ballet dancer

Javanese ear
and arm
ornaments

Costume
designs

Dancing
bodhisattva

Pointe ballet
shoes

Jewellery
for bharata
natyam

Eyewitness
DANCE

Written by
DR ANDRÉE GRAU

The fish dive,
popular in
classical ballet

DK

A Dorling Kindersley Book

DK

LONDON, NEW YORK, TORONTO,
MELBOURNE, MUNICH, and DELHI

Pointe ballet
shoes

Finger cymbals,
Morocco

Project editors Cynthia O'Neill, Marian Broderick
Art editor Cheryl Telfer
Picture research Louise Thomas
Senior managing editor Linda Martin
Senior managing art editor Julia Harris
Production Lisa Moss
DTP designer Nicky Studdart
Special photography Andy Crawford

PAPERBACK EDITION
Managing editors Linda Esposito, Andrew Macintyre
Managing art editor Jane Thomas
Category publisher Linda Martin
Art director Simon Webb
Editor and reference compiler Clare Hibbert
Art editor Joanna Pocock
Consultant Mary Schon
Production Jenny Jacoby
Picture research Celia Dearing
DTP designer Siu Yin Ho
4 6 8 10 9 7 5 3
This Eyewitness ® Guide has been conceived by
Dorling Kindersley Limited and Editions Gallimard

Hardback edition first published in Great Britain in 1998.
This edition first published in Great Britain in 2003
by Dorling Kindersley Limited,
80 Strand, London WC2R 0RL

Copyright © 1998, © 2003, Dorling Kindersley Limited, London
Penguin Group

A CIP catalogue record for this book is
available from the British Library.

ISBN 0 7513 6487 8

Colour reproduction by
Colourscan, Singapore
Printed in China by
Toppan Co., (Shenzhen) Ltd.

Metal anklet,
Ghana

Thigh bell,
Kenya

Court dancer,
Java, Indonesia

Jazz dancer, USA

See our complete
catalogue at

www.dk.com

Contents

Kathkali dancer, India

What is dance?

DANCE IS A SERIES OF MOVEMENTS, performed in patterns and set to an accompaniment. Every human society practises dance, either solo, in couples, or in groups. People around the world use dance to express themselves, pass on their history, and exercise their bodies. In this way, dance can be a celebration of the emotional, mental, and physical human self. It can also be a preparation for battle, or act as an unspoken protest. Dance is often used to mark major life changes, or to commemorate an important event in a nation's history. In the earliest societies, dance helped humans survive – it was one way for communities to learn cooperation in working and hunting together – and, as today, dance was probably used to communicate and express feelings that are difficult to convey in any other way.

Dinka folk dancer, Sudan, Africa

Steps of difficult folk dances take time to master

JOY OF DANCE
When experiencing great joy, we often feel an urge to leap and dance. For many people, Gene Kelly's exuberant dancing in the film *Singin' in the Rain* (1952) is a perfect illustration of the joy of dance.

LOST DANCES
Dances, unlike many other works of art, are not fixed in time – they exist only while being performed. Many dances, such as the galliard of the 16th century, are no longer performed, and the moves are now lost. An early engraving gives us only the faintest idea of what the galliard might have looked like.

DANCES AS A FOLK FORM
Certain dances are created by, and belong to, particular groups of people and are passed down through generations. In many parts of Africa, these dances can reinforce a people's sense of identity, or can be used to celebrate rituals or rites of passage.

DANCE AS AN ART FORM
Modern dance has generally been against the classical forms, such as ballet. However, some contemporary black dancers have retained the visual poetry of classical dance – both European and African – while mixing it with impulsive gestures from folk and street dance. This has made a new art form.

Classical leg shapes of ballet

Briefly held, statue-like poses come from the classical tradition

Modern hand movements

An"isolation" is when the trunk moves independently of other body parts

A graceful improvization from folk or street dances

Eye contact adds to the sensuality of the tango

Body shapes are perfectly symmetrical

Clothing is chosen to emphasize the swirling fluidity of jazz dance movements

BANNED DANCES
Some dances are disapproved of so much they are banned. In 1913, German army and navy personnel could be dismissed for dancing the tango. In the US in 1956, during one of Elvis Presley's first television appearances, cameras showed him only from the waist up, because the gyrating movements of his hips were considered shocking.

ORDER AND RHYTHM
In ancient Greece, dance was seen as the gift of the immortals. The Greek word, "chora", meaning "source of joy" resembles "choros", the Greek word for dance. Order and rhythm, the main qualities of dance, were also the qualities of the gods. The philosopher Plato wrote that dance "gave the body its just proportions".

Foot moves again echo the foot movements of ballet

Barefoot dancing is one way of throwing off the traditions of the past

Buddhist dancing figure, China

SACRED DANCES
Many religions, such as the Sunni Islam, use dance as a part of worship, and dancing figures are often seen in shrines of these faiths. Other religions have ritual gestures instead of dance – special movements performed by priests while reading from sacred texts, or special postures adopted while praying. In medieval times, walking the maze of Chartres Cathedral in France was part of religious worship.

Learning to dance

WE ALL LEARN to dance in our own way, whether by imitation or instruction. Different societies look for different things in a dancer's body. Some dancers, including Southeast Asian classical dancers, are expected to have a particular look. Every day they practise exercises that develop their muscles and posture in a specific way, creating an extraordinary dancer's body. Other dance styles accept a variety of body shapes and sizes, but all require great stamina and flexibility. In some places, dances are only for young people and performers retire when they reach middle age, or even before. Other societies appreciate that dancers acquire more depth in their style as they grow older.

For practice, Cambodian dancers wear comfortable clothes, but are literally sewn into their costumes in performance

Thumb and index finger create a classic offering gesture

CLASSICAL CAMBODIAN DANCE
A slow, almost hypnotic pace, and smooth wave-like movements characterize the classical dance of Cambodia. To achieve the effect, dancers need to develop a high degree of articulation, or flexibility, in all their joints. Students practise special exercises that make their fingers and elbows so supple that they appear to be without bones.

A walking step

Flexibility of the ankle joint is important as it helps dancers to move in a gliding fashion

Twists and spirals from the centre of the body form part of the dance's pattern

MARTHA GRAHAM
For Martha Graham (1894–1991), there was nothing more wonderful than the human body. She saw dance as a celebration of the miracle of the body's beauty, and she called dancers "athletes of God". Like athletes, Graham expected her dancers' movements to be disciplined, and they carried out a daily regime of taught exercises, which were based on her principles of contraction, release, and spiral. Graham's dances were designed to reveal a person's inner landscape – what she called the "cave of the heart".

The Song, choreographed by Martha Graham, 1985

DOING THE SAMBA, BRAZIL
The samba is a fast-moving dance that, like many South American dances, has African and Caribbean roots. In preparation for Rio de Janeiro's annual carnival, dancers practise for months in samba schools – neighbourhood social clubs, the main purpose of which is to organize carnival processions. A prize is awarded every year to the best samba school and competition is fierce.

Graham's dances incorporate a lot of floor work

LEARNING TO DANCE IN BALI

In Bali, Indonesia, dance lessons tend to be public occasions where everyone is free to watch. The Balinese are interested not only in dance performance but also in the entire learning process. Children learn dance forms mainly through imitation (known as nuwutin), but dance teachers also manipulate the limbs of their young students by placing them in the correct positions. Even before a child gets a teacher – maybe even before she or he can walk – their relatives will be bending their arms and hands into the correct positions.

Balinese children learn to keep their face in a tranquil, mask-like expression.

A quiet intensity and alert eyes characterize most Balinese dance

Stylized and graceful dance, such as that of Japan, suits the older dancers

Symmetry is usually an important part of Japanese dance

Arms are held at sharp angles

The gracefulness of arm and hand movements are a major part of Balinese dance

Torso is held straight with a slightly arched spine and the shoulders slightly up

OLD AND YOUNG

Dance is not the prerogative of the young – in Asia, for example, the older the dancer is, the better. Both youthful and elderly Japanese celebrate the coming of spring once a year by dancing at Sakura festivals. With the cherry-blossom trees spectacularly full of bloom, the dancers honour the beauty and short lifespan of their national flower.

Brightly coloured material is made into a sarong and wrapped around the dancer

Limbo pole is constantly lowered after each success to add a competitive element

Fire makes the dance even more of a display – and even more competitive

LIMBO DANCING

Many folk dances have a competitive element. In the Caribbean, during carnivals and other celebrations, young dancers often show off and compete with each other by performing dances that include acrobatic feats. One of these, known as the limbo dance, originated in West Africa. While it looks spontaneous, it actually requires a suppleness and agility that is built up over an extended period.

Balinese dance is performed barefoot

11

Ballet class

EACH VARIETY OF DANCE is supported by a technique that needs to be mastered by dancers. These techniques have been refined, sometimes over hundreds of years, to create an ideal of beauty. To achieve this ideal, some dancers dedicate their lives to dance, learning their skills through discipline and years of training started in childhood. For example, in classical ballet, dancers have to be elegant, long-limbed, and flexible. Although they need amazing stamina, every movement must appear effortless. Ballet dancers, no matter how exalted their position in the company, attend daily class to keep their bodies in peak condition and to maintain control over their muscles and movements.

BUILDING STRENGTH
To make difficult lifts look effortless, male dancers must be strong. As well as studying the steps, boys train with special exercises that build up their strength without making their physique too bulky. These exercises are strictly supervised.

Exercises to strengthen the upper body are important for male dancers

SCHOOLS AND COMPANIES
Prestigious ballet companies are often affiliated with ballet schools. Many dancers with the world-famous Kirov Ballet (above) began at the Kirov School in St Petersburg, Russia.

Dance pupils at the Royal Ballet School, London, UK

Dancers learn basic moves correctly at the barre

Back is straight

Knees bent over toes

Thighs horizontal to floor

1 BEGINNER'S EXERCISES
Among the first movements a beginner learns are pliés (bends) and relevés (rises). These "easy" moves must be practised many times to get them right. This is the starting position for a grand plié in second.

2 Pliés help to stretch and strengthen a dancer's leg muscles. The dancer bends smoothly and slowly into a demi-plié (half bend), with his feet turned out and his heels on the floor.

3 The dancer bends further into a grand plié (full bend), keeping his heels on the floor. He takes care to keep his movements controlled and smooth throughout.

LEARNING ARABESQUES

As dance pupils progress, they move on to more difficult movements such as the arabesque. In this beautiful position, a dancer balances on one leg with her other leg extended behind her and makes a long, slanted line with her body. Dancers are taught the basic kinds of arabesque first, such as the low arabesque, shown right.

The upper back is kept straight

Head is kept up

Front hand is turned palm down, following the line of the arm

A diagonal line is created by the left leg and the right arm

DEGAS AND THE BALLET

More than half the paintings by the French Impressionist painter Edgar Degas (1834–1917) feature young ballerinas. In his richly coloured work, the artist captured behind-the-scenes moments, such as this ballet class. The elderly teacher, leaning on his stick is, in fact, the choreographer Jules Perrot (1810–1894), who earlier in his career choreographed the romantic ballet *Giselle*.

LIFTING HIGHER

As a dancer builds up strength, she is able to lift her leg higher behind her. Her body makes a beautifully curved line from her raised foot to her shoulder, and she is perfectly balanced. Her arms stretch out softly in flowing harmony with her body.

Working leg

ADVANCED ARABESQUES

A pupil who has studied ballet for years can perform more advanced movements such as the move shown here. The dancer balances on demi-pointe. She turns her head to look over her front shoulder. In this expressive movement, the dancer can raise and lower her working leg in a sweeping motion.

Soft, flowing line

In a demi-pointe, the dancer stands on the ball of her foot

Legs appear to be crossed to the audience

Dancers hold the barre for support during certain exercises at the beginning of the class

BALLET STUDIOS

Mirrors line the walls of dance studios so that pupils can check their positions during class. The wooden floor is specially constructed to "give" slightly when dancers land from a jump. This protects their joints from uncomfortable jarring. A wooden handrail, known as a barre, runs around the wall.

ARABESQUE CROISÉ À TERRE

There is a great variety of arabesques, and ballet pupils learn how each can express different moods and feelings. In the arabesque known as croisé à terre, the dancer's back and neck make a graceful line. The dancer concentrates on maintaining the correct placing of her legs and holding her hips level.

Accompaniment to dance

DANCE USUALLY COMBINES movements with music – but not always. Sometimes dance can be accompanied by other, non-musical sounds, such as street noise, insect or animal sounds, or even the rhythmic banging of a door. Dance can also be accompanied by meaningful texts, such as beautiful or sacred poetry. It can even be performed in silence. The relationship between dance and its accompaniment varies widely but, musical or otherwise, accompaniment is vital to help establish the right atmosphere. In European and American theatre dance, for example, the orchestra is usually hidden from the audience, whereas in other parts of the world, the musicians are often on display and greatly contribute to the visual spectacle.

Drumsticks can be hit together to create another percussion sound

TONGA DANCE
Traditional sung poetry, often based on myths and legends, accompanies some dances on the Pacific island of Tonga. The dancer interprets important words in the poem. For example, if the text mentions a flower, the dance may represent a breeze carrying the flower's fragrance. The dances are usually performed standing or sitting, and include graceful hand and arm movements.

CLAPPING AND THE CUECA
In the cueca, a Chilean dance for couples, guitars provide the main accompaniment, but singers and dancers punctuate the music with handclaps. This lively dance and accompaniment inspired the song "America" in Leonard Bernstein's hit musical *West Side Story*.

DRUMMING IN AFRICA
Because Africa is a large continent with more than 50 countries, there is an immense variety of dance music, ranging from unaccompanied traditional singing to the "talking" drums of West Africa, which imitate the sounds of speech. Drum music is also especially popular in Burundi and other parts of East Africa. The drums used in large ensembles, such as this one, have to be tuned carefully because the melody is as important as the rhythm they provide.

Drum ensembles usually have a leader

Drums are tuned by tightening the wooden screws

Animal hide stretched over tree trunk

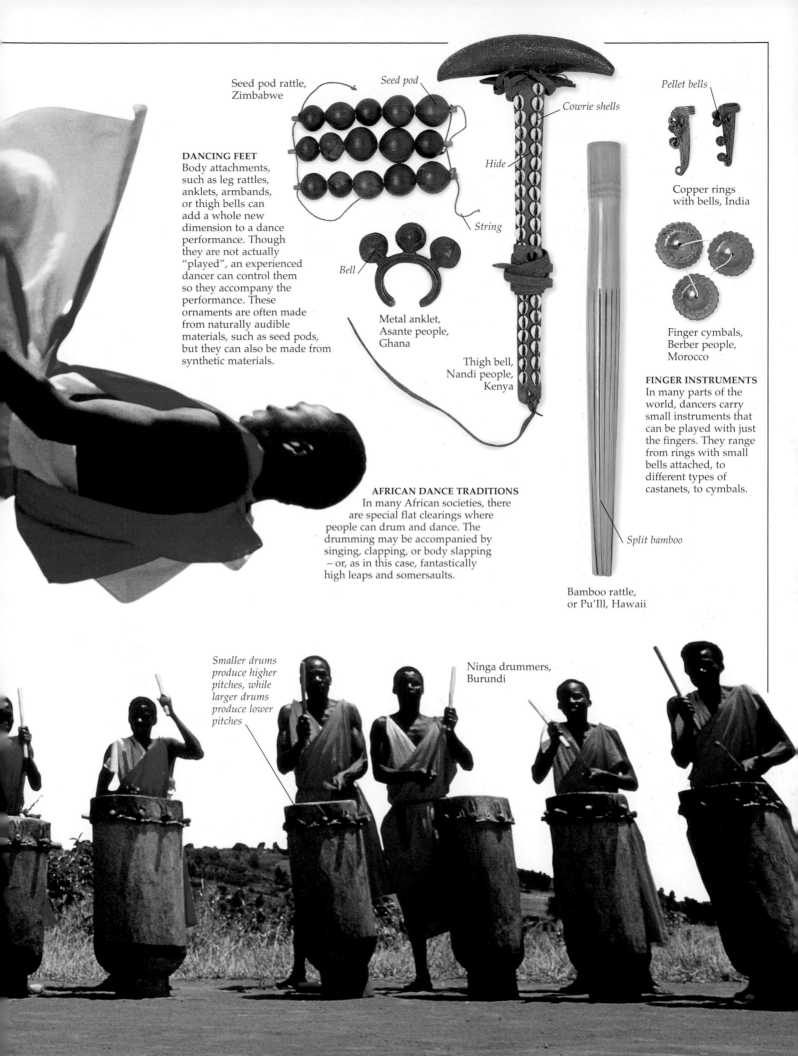

Seed pod rattle,
Zimbabwe

Seed pod

Cowrie shells

Hide

String

Bell

Pellet bells

**Copper rings
with bells, India**

DANCING FEET
Body attachments,
such as leg rattles,
anklets, armbands,
or thigh bells can
add a whole new
dimension to a dance
performance. Though
they are not actually
"played", an experienced
dancer can control them
so they accompany the
performance. These
ornaments are often made
from naturally audible
materials, such as seed pods,
but they can also be made from
synthetic materials.

Metal anklet,
Asante people,
Ghana

Thigh bell,
Nandi people,
Kenya

**Finger cymbals,
Berber people,
Morocco**

FINGER INSTRUMENTS
In many parts of the
world, dancers carry
small instruments that
can be played with just
the fingers. They range
from rings with small
bells attached, to
different types of
castanets, to cymbals.

AFRICAN DANCE TRADITIONS
In many African societies, there
are special flat clearings where
people can drum and dance. The
drumming may be accompanied by
singing, clapping, or body slapping
– or, as in this case, fantastically
high leaps and somersaults.

Split bamboo

Bamboo rattle,
or Pu'Ill, Hawaii

*Smaller drums
produce higher
pitches, while
larger drums
produce lower
pitches*

Ninga drummers,
Burundi

Keeping time

WE ALL HAVE A SENSE of ourselves and of other people moving through space and time. In dancers, this sense is highly developed. Dancers are aware of their bodies and of the effect of their movements on an audience. When they are carrying out one action, they are mentally anticipating the next; they subtly adjust their movements towards the following step, preparing the audience for the next image. Performers use rhythm to achieve this kind of exchange with an audience. Rhythm is a timing system that develops on a basic pattern of silences and pauses. Performers cannot ignore the laws of rhythm, and cannot dance without a sense of rhythm, but they can carve out their own way of interpreting it. Whether it is the fast, exciting rhythms of the flamenco of Spain, or the slow, controlled rhythms of Japanese noh, successful dancers create their own timing on top of a basic rhythmic pattern.

TIWI PEOPLE, AUSTRALIA
Among the Tiwi aboriginal people of Melville and Bathurst islands, clear lines and rhythm are essential for movements to be considered dance. They specialize in "strong dancing", where every change must occur exactly on the beat. Movements flowing across the rhythm exist in the Tiwi repertoire, but they are performed only as song gestures.

Sumptuous costumes are made of gold and silver brocade

Masks used in noh are an art form in themselves

NOH DANCERS
The Japanese dance-drama noh is a majestic and beautiful art form. The gestures, breathing, and music in each scene of each performance are underlined by the complex idea of *Jo-ha-kyu*, which concerns the rhythmic relationship between two forces pulling in opposite directions. Noh is very slow-moving, and performances are extremely long. It has been compared to watching a flower change imperceptibly and eventually shed its petals.

Noh relies on symbolism, often provided by props

Kathak dancers occasionally dance in pairs

KATHAK
In Indian music, rhythm is expressed by tal, a system of beats that gives a dance its structure. The dancers of kathak, an energetic dance form from northern India, are expert at improvizing intricate steps with their feet while making graceful movements with their arms. Kathak dancers are involved in a "conversation" with musicians, which develops as the performance goes on. They explore the cycle of beats individually, but at key moments of the music cycle they synchronize their timing.

FOUR TEMPERAMENTS

Listening to some music, George Balanchine (1904–83) was moved "to try to make visible not only the rhythm, melody, and harmony but even the timbres [tones] of the instruments." In 1946, he set a ballet to Paul Hindemith's *The Four Temperaments* that tried to represent, through pure dance, what was in the composer's mind musically.

The Four Temperaments, 1946

A scene from Choerartium (1933)

FLAMENCO

The origins of the flamboyant Spanish dance known as flamenco are obscure. Some say flamenco originated in the southern province of Andalusia. Others say it came to Andalusia with gypsies who travelled from India and Pakistan via Egypt, and that the roots of flamenco are in the kathak. In both the flamenco and the kathak, sophisticated footwork creates rhythmic patterns and the dance itself acts as percussion. Improvization may still be practised in both, and dialogue with the musicians is crucial in both.

Elegant arm and hand movements of flamenco are sometimes reinforced with the use of a fan

Performers manipulate their costumes as part of the dance

SYMPHONIC BALLET

In the 1930s, the Russian choreographer Léonide Massine created a number of ballets set to symphonies. *Choreartium,* which was set to Brahms' Fourth Symphony, was his second. Although other choreographers had previously arranged ballets to symphonies, they were isolated productions. Debate raged around Massine's work – some people felt that dancing to symphonic music somehow debased the symphony.

Castanets are not a traditional part of flamenco but are used in the folk dances of southern Spain

Musicians sometimes hit the wood of the guitar to add another percussive sound

FLAMENCO AND ACCOMPANIMENT

The three main components in flamenco are singing (cante), dancing (baile), and guitar (guitarra). Performances originally included only singing and dancing, with some hand-clapping (toque de palmas). The guitar came later, first as accompaniment then as a solo instrument in its own right.

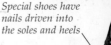

Special shoes have nails driven into the soles and heels

Themes and messages

DANCE DOES NOT ALWAYS SIMPLY tell a story. It may be used to bring people together, by reinforcing their shared beliefs about their place in the world and their relationship with the supernatural. Some dances, such as the Native American Ghost Dance, were created to channel frustration and bring hope for the future. Others, such as the haka of New Zealand, are war dances that can raise aggression against enemies. Some communal African dances teach the the young the values of society by showing the path they are expected to follow. In contrast, other dances, such as modern anti-war ballets, challenge society's values and bring new ideas.

Club represents the owner's supernatural helper

Arapaho ghost dance club, 1800s

GHOST DANCE
This dance was a response by the Native Americans of the Great Plains to intolerable poverty and oppression. Carrying carved clubs, they danced in appeal to their gods to restore traditional ways, and bring back the buffalo. The dance was banned by the white authorities.

DANCING AGAINST WAR
With his ballet *The Green Table* (1932), Kurt Jooss tried to move people to take action against the evil political system of fascism, which was overtaking Europe in the 1930s. The ballet is about the two-faced nature of some diplomats, and how they must shoulder the responsibility for the deaths caused by war.

Kurt Jooss

Masks worn by the dancers

BUFFALO DANCE
The buffalo dance, as shown in this 19th-century painting, carries a message of respect for the animals that are about to be killed. For instance, the Blackfoot promised the buffalo that life taken from it in this world would be returned in the next. They believed that a sacred ritual dance had the power to make this happen.

Buffalo heads worn during the dance

Dancers enter a hypnotic state

Shouting and warlike gestures accompany the haka

Traditional wooden weapons are used as part of the haka

DANCING FOR WAR
Throughout the world, dance has been used to drill warriors, both as a way of strengthening their muscles in preparation for hand-to-hand combat, and to unify the fighters. The Maori people of New Zealand traditionally performed a war dance, known as the haka, before battle and in victory celebrations afterwards. Today, New Zealand rugby teams prepare for their matches in world competition by performing the haka before kick-off.

GREAT DOMBA SONG

Among the Venda of South Africa, young women prepare for marriage and their integration into adult life by learning the milayos – laws set out in poems and riddles – and dancing the domba. The tight chain of the domba requires very good timing and cooperation.

HARVESTS AND CROPS

Dances are performed at harvest festival around the world to celebrate the end of a successful farming year. The ritual is thought to help regenerate the earth in preparation for the next harvest. Such dances also promote social unity and cooperation in the face of the dangers and whims of nature.

Ankle or shin bells add to the rhythm of the dance

The colours blue and yellow represent a town called Letchworth in the heart of England

Fresh flowers adorn hats to represent spring and regeneration

MORRIS COSTUME

Morris dancers emphasize group unity by dressing alike. They wear white shirts, flowered straw hats, and braces, known as baldricks. Morris costume sometimes includes bells attached to the shin that ring in time with the movements of the dance.

MORRIS DANCE

Traditionally performed at local festivals in the South Midlands of England, morris dancing is performed today throughout the country. It was once an exclusively male ceremonial dance, but now is danced by amateurs of both sexes – often in competitions. Categories of the dances include processional, jig, and set dancing. Team dancing is deliberately boisterous – this reinforces team spirit among the participants, especially when in competition.

Sticks or handkerchiefs are often used

Baldricks

Team colours

Telling tales

Firebird is dressed in red

This move is designed to indicate struggle – the prince is forcing the firebird to help him

DANCE TELLS STORIES in many ways. Some dances use mime, facial expression, and movements that have specific meanings. For example, in southern India, kathakali performers use a code of gesture that literally translates the text sung by an accompanying vocalist. Often, however, dance uses stories that are already well-known. Western audiences know the story of *Sleeping Beauty* from childhood, while Indian children are taught the many mischievous adventures of the god Krishna, his ways with milkmaids, and his love for the beautiful Rhada. In every society, people watch dance because it has the power to bring a special interpretation to these popular tales. The very deepest human emotions – love, betrayal, despair – can all be expressed in dance.

BURMESE PUPPET
In the puppet theatres of Southeast Asia, well-known stories are told by Burmese string marionettes – like the one above – Indonesian shadow puppets, and Vietnamese water puppets.

FIGHT BETWEEN GOOD AND EVIL
Ballet stories are often about love winning against cruelty and malice. In *The Firebird* (1910), a magical bird of fire helps Prince Ivan rescue a beautiful princess and rid the world of an evil magician known as Kostchei.

Prince Albrecht wooing Giselle

Giselle plucking a daisy

Iconic gesture of flute-playing always represents the god Krishna

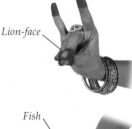

Lion-face

Fish

BHARATA NATYAM
The classical Indian dance form bharata natyam blends two very different but complementary types of movements: expressive dance, which interprets classical poetry through mime, and abstract dance with rhythmic improvization. Hand gestures and stylized facial expressions (abhinaya) are crucial.

ELOQUENT HANDS
Hand gestures in bharata natyam are known as hasta or mudras. Some hand gestures are iconic – they look like what they represent. Others are symbolic – they are abstract gestures.

STORY OF GISELLE
The ballet *Giselle* (1841) tells of a simple village girl overwhelmed by the attention of Albrecht, a prince disguised as a peasant. When Giselle discovers that Albrecht has deceived her and is already engaged, she goes mad and dies of a broken heart. She joins the Wilis, the spirits of young girls betrayed in love. In Act I, Giselle's symbolic movements, such as playing he-loves-me-he-loves-me-not with a flower, emphasize her innocence.

EXPRESSING EMOTION THROUGH DANCE
A pas de deux in ballet is a dance for two performers, usually a man and a woman. It presents a relationship – often a beautiful vision of romantic love – from its first awakening to the great joy of its realization. The dancing of a pas de deux can be intimate, or extravagant and full of passion. Between sections of dancing together, each performer traditionally performs a solo dance, known as a variation, showing his and her individuality.

This arabesque penché (bent forward) is one of the most beautiful expressions of romantic love

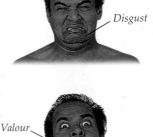

Disgust

Valour

KATHAKALI
Performers of this Indian dance form develop phenomenal control over their facial muscles, eyes, and lower and upper eyelids. Through stylized facial expressions, a huge range of emotions, such as valour, revulsion, love, anger, compassion, derision, wonder, and fear can be conveyed to the audience.

Costumes contribute to the successful telling of a story

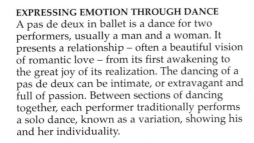

Male dancers always look at the ballerina

Strong knees and thighs are essential for supporting and lifting

Dancers train from childhood to achieve great strength yet softness in the hands

Serene expression is part of the dance choreography

CELESTIAL NYMPH
Thai dancers, like Indian dancers, tell of the heroic mythological beings from the *Ramayana*, an ancient epic poem. However, unlike the Indian hastas, Thai hand gestures do not tell the story literally, but are designed to add beauty and grace to the overall shape of a dance.

Fingers, palms, and wrists contribute to the overall shape of the dance

Beauty and strength

PEOPLE EVERYWHERE TAKE PLEASURE in beautiful objects, music, and dance. Yet what is seen as graceful or lovely in one place can be thought ugly or inappropriate in another. For example, it is shocking for a traditional Indonesian audience to see a ballerina extend her legs, because in Indonesian dance women do not display their legs in this way. Around the world, there are many different sets of rules that decide "good" and "bad" taste. All the members of a community share these rules – but occasionally artists adapt or disregard them to introduce new ideas and overcome boundaries.

JAVANESE COURT DANCER, INDONESIA
At the sultan's court on the Indonesian island of Java, there is a pure dance style called bedoyo, which is performed only by women. The Javanese court dancer must seem to move smoothly and effortlessly. Her graceful, rolling movements are thought to represent the spiritual refinement and wisdom of kingship.

Gilt-edged sampur

Gentle angles and slow movements convey the serenity and elegance of the dance

ROYAL RWANDANS
The royal Tutsi dancers of Rwanda re-enact past heroic deeds. This dance commemorates the courageous defence of the kingdom from cattle raiders. The dancers try to represent the vigour and nobility of an ideal warrior. They symbolize the king's authority and are accompanied by the royal drums.

Legs are kept hidden in Indonesian dance

Hair ornament

Ear ornament

ADORNMENTS
Javanese dancers wear delicate jewellery and accessories, including ear ornaments made from gilded buffalo-hide! Their dancing also contains stylized gestures such as playing with earrings or adjusting a head ornament.

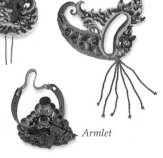

Armlet

FLOWING WATER
Female classical dancers on Java embody the Javanese ideals of beauty, becoming behaviour, and spiritual growth. In both dance and life, Javanese custom has it that a woman's movements should be quiet, restrained, and modest – and as calming as flowing water. The flow of water is also reflected in choreography: dance movements constantly fill the space the way water would fill a vessel. This dancer gently waves her sampur to emphasize the grace and flow of her movements.

Feet are kept close together, and stay in contact with the floor

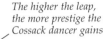

The higher the leap, the more prestige the Cossack dancer gains

COSSACK LEAPS
In many societies, men often have the exclusive use of high jumps. Russian soldiers known as Cossacks, for example, use their vital dance style to show off their agility, physical prowess, and technical skills. The Cossacks like to compete for prestige by outdoing each other's acrobatic feats.

MALE DANCER, JAVA, INDONESIA
Unlike female dancers, whose feet scarcely lose contact with the floor, Javanese male dancers – often depicting warriors – execute wide, sweeping movements and postures. Similarly, while the focus for a female dancer's eyes is generally limited to the floor for a distance of two to five steps, the forceful male dancer can extend the focus of his eyes forward to a distance three times his height.

Ornate gilded ear ornaments

The heroes of one popular dance-drama, the Ramayana, *are often portrayed as archers*

The tilted torso gives the illusion that the arrow is being shot

Leg lifted so thigh is parallel with the floor

Heroic dance often features traditional weapons, such as a sword, as part of the costume

Brown is one of the most popular colours used in Javanese costume

HIGHLAND LEAPS
While some dance forms are "earthed", almost caressing the ground, others use high leaps that seem to defy gravity. Scottish Highland dance emphasizes both elevation and swift foot movements, which contrast sharply with the stiffness of the upper body.

Hands are together in a gesture of reverence

Sharp angles created by arms

CREATING A WARRIOR
This Javanese dancer achieves a regal and martial posture by straightening his body, forcing his wrists and elbows into sharp angles, and creating another wide angle with his knee. In contrast to western ballet's extended foot, Javanese dancers tense the toes upward.

Wide leg gestures are acceptable for male dancers

Weight-bearing leg is kept straight

Foot must be turned out sideways

23

Fancy footwear

MOST DANCE STYLES depend on the way dancers use their feet. Whether shaped by special shoes or left free, dancers' feet determine their basic posture and movements. The development of ballet shoes shows how footwear and dance styles influence each other. Until the 1810s, ballerinas wore simple slippers and kept the balls of their feet in contact with the floor. However, audiences wanted ballerinas to seem as light as air, and this led to dancing en pointe (on the tip of the toes). To dance this way, ballerinas relied on specially constructed reinforced shoes.

TIPPY-TOES
Since its invention in the 1810s, dancing en pointe has been identified with classical ballet techniques.

Pink, red, and orange were all tango colours

TANGO BOOTS, 1910s
When the tango craze hit Europe in the early 20th century, dancers opted for boots in hot "tango colours".

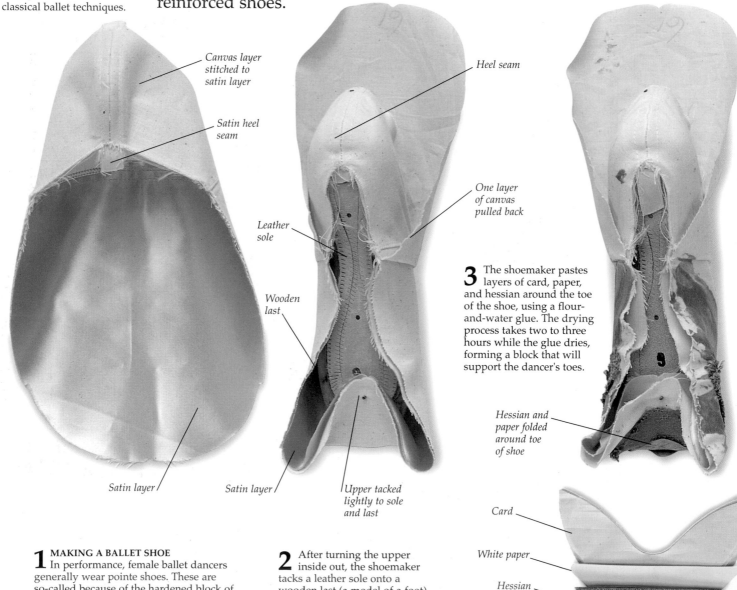

Canvas layer stitched to satin layer

Satin heel seam

Heel seam

One layer of canvas pulled back

Leather sole

Wooden last

Satin layer

Satin layer

Upper tacked lightly to sole and last

3 The shoemaker pastes layers of card, paper, and hessian around the toe of the shoe, using a flour-and-water glue. The drying process takes two to three hours while the glue dries, forming a block that will support the dancer's toes.

Hessian and paper folded around toe of shoe

Card

White paper

Hessian

Different thicknesses of grey paper

1 MAKING A BALLET SHOE
In performance, female ballet dancers generally wear pointe shoes. These are so-called because of the hardened block of hessian and paper that allows the dancer to dance en pointe. Despite the delicate appearance of the satin upper, these shoes are stiff. The shoemaker begins the shoe by stitching together satin and canvas layers to make the upper.

2 After turning the upper inside out, the shoemaker tacks a leather sole onto a wooden last (a model of a foot). He then pulls the inside-out upper onto the last, and peels back one layer of canvas. The shoemaker tacks the upper to the last, through the leather sole.

Ankle bells accompany the dancer as she stamps her feet

PLATFORM SOLES
Performers in traditional dance forms, such as Japanese kabuki or Chinese opera, wear shoes with elevated soles. Platforms have also been popular in more informal contexts, such as the disco fashions of the 1970s.

Platform soles decorated with rhinestones

Stilt dancer, Ivory Coast

PAINTED FEET
In bharata natyam, a classical Indian dance style, performers decorate their feet instead of wearing shoes. The designs complement the patterns painted on their hands.

Designs painted on with henna emphasizes the curved lines of the feet

STILT DANCERS
In areas of southern and western Africa, dancers perform on stilts up to two metres (six feet) high. Leg-crossing, jumps, and twirls are precarious, but that is partly the point of the stilt dance. Finding the right balance symbolizes the wisdom of humankind.

Heel

Shoe turned right side out

Leather insole

Drawstring

Sole is stitched to upper

Layer of canvas is pulled forward to cover the paper-and-glue block

Dancers soften new shoes to shape them to their feet — some soften shoes by closing them in a door!

Wax thread

Canvas is stitched in tight pleats around the block

Shoemaker's mark

4 When the glue has dried, the peeled-back layer of canvas is pulled forward and pleated around the toe with metal pincers. The shoemaker stitches the hard leather sole to the upper, using wax thread. The shoe is removed from the last, and turned the right way out. A leather insole is then inserted before the shoe is put back on the last.

5 The shoemaker shapes and fashions the shoe with a special smooth hammer. This tool is also used to shape the pointe into a platform. Finally, the finished shoes are put into a warm oven to harden for 12 to 15 hours, or overnight.

Satin ribbons, normally about 2.5 cm (1 in) wide and 50 cm (1.5 ft) long

6 Traditionally, dancers sew the ribbons onto their own shoes and often embroider the toe area to stop the fabric from fraying. Pointe shoes have a remarkably short life; principal dancers in a ballet company wear out about a dozen pairs a month!

Make-up

THROUGHOUT THE WORLD, performers apply make-up to dramatize their features. Whether they use ochres, charcoal, synthetic materials, or paints made from powdered stones, make-up has many uses. It highlights beauty; transforms humans into heroes, demons, or animals; or acts as a mask, hiding a dancer's identity. In India, kathakali performers use make-up to transform themselves into mythical beings. In Africa, Woodabe men use make-up and dance to express their inner beauty.

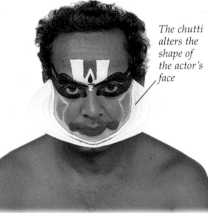

Traditional make-up is applied with an erkila, a stick made from a stripped coconut leaf

1 APPLYING KATHAKALI MAKE-UP
In kathakali, a dance-drama from South India, an artist applies layers of make-up. The colourful and elaborate designs, which take up to four hours to complete, have been handed down over centuries.

The chutti alters the shape of the actor's face

CHINESE OPERA
In Chinese opera, make-up defines characters and covers the actor's whole face. Until early in the 20th century, men performed all the roles – even that of beautiful princesses!

Eyebrows are strongly defined, as they are an essential element of beauty

A princess is made up in white, red, and shades of pink

"STILL LIFE" AT THE PENGUIN CAFÉ
The stunning costumes and make-up used in the modern ballet *Still Life at the Penguin Café* helped to reinforce its ecological message about endangered species.

2 ATTACHING THE CHUTTI
One of the most distinctive aspects of kathakali make-up is the chutti – a white "frame" that focuses the audience's attention on the actor's face. Traditionally, the make-up artist constructs the chutti from specially cut paper and inserts it into layers of rice paste. Applying the chutti takes at least an hour.

Dancers dust their faces with yellow powder

A special seed, the chundapoo, is washed, cut, and inserted into the eyelid to make the eyes look bloodshot

BEAUTY CONTESTS FOR MEN
The Woodabe people of Niger, West Africa, hold dancing competitions so the women can decide which man is the most attractive. A contestant uses make-up to emphasize his eyes, his long, thin nose, and his white teeth, and he pulls facial expressions to show off his inner beauty.

DRESSING ROOM
Backstage at the ballet, dancers make themselves up in dressing rooms shared out according to rank: the more important the dancer, the bigger their dressing room. The *corps de ballet* share a space, but principal dancers have their own rooms and often their own make-up artists.

3 MAKING THE EYES RED
When the chutti is dry, the actor applies the rest of his make-up. As a final touch, he cuts a seed known as a chundapoo and inserts it into his eyelid. The cut seed 'dyes the white of the eye red, and this highlights the expressive eye movements that are a major part of a kathakali performance.

The heavy kiritam (headdress) is made of wood and inlaid with imitation gemstones

SPECTACLE OF KATHAKALI

Kathakali narrates the heroic adventures from India's two most famous epics, the *Mahabharata* and the *Ramayana*. Dealing with the constant struggle between good and evil, kathakali is highly spectacular and often involves a fierce battle that results in the destruction of a supernatural demon. The ornaments, movements, and especially the costumes and make-up emphasize the sacred nature of the characters. Noble-hearted heroes always have green faces, while actors playing treacherous schemers paint their faces dark red or black.

Coconut shell, holding rice paste

Spirit gum

Erkila

Chutti coil

Paper to make chutti

Paints

COLOURS AND TOOLS

Rocks are ground up and mixed with coconut oil to produce the vivid paints used by kathakali actors. Spirit gum and then rice paste are applied with a chutti coil to paste the chutti paper to the actor's face.

The kiritam is usually painted in red, green, white, and gold

The eyebrows and eyes are exaggerated with black make-up

ABORIGINAL DREAMTIME

In parts of Australia, Aboriginal dancers apply ochre and soft feathers to their bodies in geometrical designs. The designs and make-up have great religious importance, linking the dancers to their ancestor spirits and to Dreamtime – the time of Creation.

Costumes in dance

DANCE COSTUMES ENHANCE A PERFORMANCE in a wide variety of ways. For example, in traditions where there are no stage sets, costumes help the audience make sense of what is going on. Costumes often follow specific codes; for example, the size of a headdress or the length of a sleeve may say something about the character. Costumes can be stunning in themselves, but their impact is usually reinforced with make-up, music, and gesture. This immediately helps an audience tell the loyal from the treacherous, the good from the wicked, and the admirable from the despicable. Costumes can veil, obstruct, round out, or emphasize the contour of the dancers' bodies and movements. They add a whole new dimension to dance.

Warriors often have long pheasant feathers in their headdress

Graceful movements of the pheasant feathers are part of the dancer's gestures

Noh kimono, Japan

Opaque tights highlight the beautiful line of the leg

CHINESE OPERA
In Chinese opera, warriors are important characters. They bring visual excitement with their acrobatic moves. Both male (wusheng) and female (wudan) warriors wear costumes that allow for ease of movement. Trousers are worn so that spectacular high kicks can be performed.

Modern transparent material

ALL-IN-ONE COSTUMES
Choreographers of western contemporary dance, like Maurice Béjart of France, focus upon the expressive power of movement. The all-in-one costume used in his work *Malraux* allows the spectators to see all the movements of the choreography.

HISTORICAL COSTUME
Costumes can indicate historical periods without being accurate historical representations. In Yolande Snaith's *Gorgeous Creatures*, the main character is recognizably Elizabeth I of England. While her clothing is inspired by the period, it is made of modern material that allows for interesting dance movements.

28

NOH DRAMA, JAPAN
The kimono (left), worn in noh, transforms the proportions of the performer's body. The wide sleeves create a contrast between the overall pyramid shape and the narrowness of the wrists. In performance, a belt is placed well above the waist.

PAVLOVA'S DYING SWAN
Michel Fokine's *La mort du cygne* (1905) became associated with Anna Pavlova just as, generations before, the name of Marie Taglioni conjured up a vision of *La Sylphide.* Rumour has it that Pavlova's last words were about the dance, and that she died clutching her costume (right).

Real swan feathers made the costume realistic

Colourful, hand-embroidered motifs

GEORGIAN BALLET
Dancers of the Republic of Georgia wear very long costumes that hide their feet. When they move they seem to glide across the floor as if mounted on wheels, and the audience cannot see how the effect is achieved.

Headdress size and design is determined by the role

Light, flowing material

Red jacket symbolizes a heroic role, while demons wear black and Lord Krishna wears dark blue

Skirt is supported by many layers of cotton underskirts

Masquerade costume, Nigeria

IBO MASQUERADE COSTUME
Masquerade costumes hide the identity of the performer. Often padding is sewn in to exaggerate or create additional body parts. This costume is worn by the Ibo men of Nigeria, West Africa, who imitate young girls as part of the annual harvest celebrations. Traditionally, a mask completes the masquerade outfit.

KATHAKALI COSTUME
Kathakali performers wear extremely ornate clothing. The colour of the jacket depends on the character, and the jacket is open at the back so that the performer can be cooled by fanning. The vast skirt is made up of many layers of white cotton, with a decorated top layer. The performer varies the skirt's length by splaying his knees and legs.

Outside of the foot bears the weight

Costume design

COSTUMES ARE AN IMPORTANT part of dance. In some traditions they act as a moving set – against a bare backdrop, they help place the characters in context. Costumes may complement or enlarge the movements of dance. In Chinese classical dance, performers wear long sleeves, which they manipulate to create beautiful shapes, while in Javanese classical dance and Spanish flamenco, female dancers kick back their trains in distinctive ways. Some costumes have ancient origins: in India, the costumes of modern classical dancers are based on temple sculptures. Since costumes are part of tradition, they often do not need re-designing, although they can be adapted to make the most of modern technology. It is quicker to use Velcro as a fastening, for instance, than hooks and buttons. In other traditions, such as in western theatre dance, where innovation is highly valued, dance costumes are regularly redesigned.

Vividly coloured stripes resemble sunrise

Wide-sleeved coat

CHINESE CONJUROR
The Chinese conjuror is one of the main characters in *Parade* (1917), a comic ballet that satirizes a troupe of entertainers. Picasso's sketches for the magician's costume are outlandish, matching the tone of the ballet.

PICASSO'S DESIGNS
Pablo Picasso (1881–1973), one of the greatest artists of the 20th century, designed costumes for the ballet. From 1917, he worked with the Ballet Russes in Paris. Many of his first costumes for the ballet *Parade* were influenced by cubism, a style of modern art that Picasso founded. The costumes caused a sensation at the time.

Early costume designs for a lead ballerina

Rich but sombre colours hint at melancholy theme of ballet

Sample costume fabrics

1 DESIGNING FOR THE BALLET
At the start of the design process, the artistic director briefs the costume designer on the production. For example, the ballet might have a melancholy atmosphere in Act III, and the costumes should reflect this. The designer then sketches early ideas. With some ballets, certain traditions must be observed: in a classical ballet, such as *Sleeping Beauty*, lead ballerinas always wear short costumes known as tutus. With newer ballets, designers can be more flexible.

Paper patterns for costume

2 MAKING THE COSTUME
The designer sketches ideas for every costume that will appear in the ballet. Once the director approves these ideas, the designer turns them into patterns – guides for cutting the fabric, usually made of paper or card. The costume is then sewn, with alterations being made after it has been fitted to the dancer.

Headdress of twisted gold echoes details of lace on cloak

Motif of vine leaves and grapes

Synthetic pearls form clusters of grapes

ALL IN THE DETAIL
In major ballet productions, even the costumes for lesser characters are designed with great detail. The Cavalier of the Golden Vine is a minor character in the ballet *Sleeping Beauty*. Nonetheless, this costume from a 1946 production is lovingly embroidered, even though it would be almost impossible to see the details from the auditorium!

Heavy cloak leaves dancer's arms free for expressive movement

Cloak is removed and hung up to become part of the set

4 USES FOR COSTUME
When Eurydice first appears to Orpheus, she is weighed down with a heavy cloak. Since it is obviously uncomfortable for a dancer to perform in a heavy costume, the costume is designed so that the ballerina can remove the cloak after the initial impact of its appearance.

3 INTO THE UNDERWORLD
When Adonais Ballet Company decided to put on the new ballet *Orpheus*, costumes were commissioned that would reflect the story. The ballet is based on the Greek myth of the musician Orpheus, who is overcome with grief when his new wife Eurydice is killed, and descends to the dark shadows of the underworld to find her. Eurydice's costume helps to show that she is now a spirit, trapped in this gloomy realm.

5 PERFORMANCE
The dancer now performs in leotard and chiffon wrap. The wispy drapes still suggest the spirit world, but do not weigh the dancer down. The costume shows off her technique; here, the chiffon highlights the beautiful shape of the arabesque.

Behind a mask

A DANCER'S FACE is one of the most expressive parts of the body, yet there are dances all over the world in which performers prefer to use masks to cover their faces. By concealing themselves behind a mask, performers can let go of their own identity and devote themselves completely to the movement. Wearing a mask challenges dancers to use their body in a particular way, so that every part of it becomes more expressive. In addition, masks can have a symbolic meaning: they may represent spirits or gods, dead ancestors, or the prized skills of a highly respected animal. Wearing a mask allows a performer to take on the special qualities of someone – or something – else.

LITTLE OLD MEN DANCE MASKS, MEXICO
Clown-like figures are part of many mask traditions. In the Mexican state of Michoacan, wooden masks painted pink represent the *Viejito*, or Little Old Man, a grandfather cavorting around in a humorous manner.

WAR DANCE, PAPUA NEW GUINEA
Men performing a war dance wear frightening masks, carry weapons, and cover their bodies with mud. Their dance represents the eternal battle between good and evil, light and darkness.

Carved skulls add to the drama of the dance

Mask is lavishly gilded with gold leaf

Papier-mâché is moulded and then painted

TIBETAN MOUNTAIN DANCERS
In the Himalaya Mountains, dancers wear wooden masks painted in bright colours (left). The performers, moving in slow rhythm in time to deep-sounding drums, dance both on festive occasions and at times of ill-fortune. Masks like this represent the spirits of their mountain gods.

Boldly coloured geometric designs

IBAN DAYAK, SARAWAK, BORNEO
The Iban Dayak, Sarawak's largest native group, traditionally use painted wooden masks (left) at harvest festivals, when dancers celebrate the end of the harvest and the fertility of the land. These dances also celebrate the connection between Iban Dayak society and the cycle of the natural world.

FÊTE DE MASQUES, CÔTE D'IVOIRE
West African countries are famous for their mask dances. Masks are usually worn to conceal the identity of the performer. The Côte d'Ivoire (Ivory Coast) has a festival of masks every year.

Bar supplies
leverage to
pull open
the beak

Mask has a dual
purpose: to represent
the eagle and to
reveal the human

RANGDA MASK, BALI, INDONESIA
According to Hindu tradition, wives were killed when
their husbands died. In Balinese dance, the unpopular
rangda, or widow figure, represents women that
survived. The witch-like rangda possesses
dangerous magical powers – only the
strongest performer can
withstand her spirit.

Rangda is
depicted
as shaggy
and wild

Drawstring
pulls the
mask aside
to reveal the
human face
beneath

Rangda has fangs
and a long, hanging
tongue to devour
children

KWAKIUTL
Among the Kwakiutl of
the American Northwest,
traditional priest-doctors
called shamans often wear
masks during ceremonies.
These connect the shamans with
the powers of their ancestors. The
masks often represent admired
creatures, such as the eagle
depicted here.

COURT DANCE, THAILAND
In Thai court dances, beautifully
ornate papier-mâché masks,
featuring an elaborate golden top,
are worn by male dancers at court
to celebrate special occasions such
as the king's birthday. Although
Thailand is a Buddhist country, court
dances usually depict one of the great
Hindu epics. One such, the *Ramayana*,
relates the heroic deeds of the god
Vishnu in his disguise as Rama, the
king of Ayodhya.

Realistic
costumes
and masks

ANIMAL MASKS
For a ballet based on the the tales of Beatrix Potter,
costumes and masks – neatly arranged in the Royal Ballet's
storeroom when not in use – recreated each animal character in minute detail.
Although the masks and costumes were inhibiting, the dancers transmitted
the personality of each character – the delightful Squirrel Nutkin, for example
– through their movements, which were brilliantly choreographed by the
British dancer and choreographer Frederick Ashton (1904–1988).

Dance and worship

Expressive eyes and hands are most important

DANCE BRINGS TOGETHER thoughts and feelings, and can create special, deeply felt emotions. In some areas of the world, such as Australia, India, Africa, and parts of western Asia, certain dances are linked to religion and are regarded as sacred: to those dancers, dancing is a form of prayer. Even in places where dance is not connected with worship, dancers say that the experience can be transcendental – in other words, it is a way to leave everyday life behind and enter a more spiritual realm.

AN ANCIENT ART
In India, practically all performing arts have close links with religion. Bharata natyam is linked to ancient temple dances in Tamil Nadu, southern India. The dancers came from special families and were known as devadasis.

This dance movement closely resembles one of the popular postures of Siva, the Indian lord of the dance

DEVADASIS IN THE COMMUNITY
In traditional Indian society, secular and religious activities were not clearly separated. Devadasis and their dances were important for rituals such as weddings, as well as for entertainment in royal courts.

WHIRLING DERVISHES
The dervishes are Muslim friars, originally from Turkey. When dancing, they spin around faster and faster with their arms spread out – until eventually they enter a trance-like state. In this higher state of mind, they believe it is possible to be in contact with God.

Pleats are practical as well as beautiful

Necklace

Anklet

Hair ornament

Anklets add percussion to the moves

DANCING TO REACH THE DREAMTIME
In Australia, Aboriginal people dance as a way of reaching a timeless zone they call the Dreamtime. According to ancient belief, this was when the universe and everything in it was created. Dancing the sacred dances recreates the universe and helps keep everything in its proper order.

COSTUME AND JEWELLERY
When bharata natyam was reconstructed in the 1930s, the costume was based on temple sculptures and everyday life. Most Hindu statues are adorned with jewellery, so this became part of the look. Since devadasis used to be dedicated to the temple god by being symbolically married to him, the costume has become popular with brides.

Ornaments and jewellery resemble those of a bride in Tamil Nadu, India

MOVING THROUGH SPACE
When performing in a confined space, bharata natyam dancers suggest space through the use of their body, particularly their eyes, rather than through large movements across a floor.

BHARATA NATYAM TODAY
Today, bharata natyam is performed in theatres as a solo concert dance. The modern art form combines elements of mood, music, and drama. The term comes from joining together parts of the words Bhava (emotion), Raga (melody), Tala (rhythm), and Natya (drama). The expressiveness of the dancer, rather than her pure athletic ability, is bharata natyam's most important quality. Although dancers are no longer married to the gods, bharata natyam is often based on stories of gods, goddesses, and heavenly nymphs. A performance always begins and ends with a dedication to God.

Hand shapes and movements are precise

Ogun, the god of iron, blacksmiths, and war

DANCE STAFF, NIGERIA
The Yoruba of Nigeria use iron dance staffs to mark the distinctive rhythms for dances associated with individual gods. Each staff is connected to a particular god.

Jewellery and flowers make the dancer resemble Hindu statues

Circle of fire

Medieval bronze of Siva Nataraja

LORD OF THE DANCE
Siva Nataraja, the Indian lord of the dance, is just one aspect of the great Hindu god Siva. The four-armed Siva Nataraja is always shown dancing. He represents the creation-death-regeneration cycle of the universe.

A demon crushed by Siva

RUTH ST DENIS
Ruth St Denis (1877–1968), one of the pioneers of American modern dance, sought to celebrate the spiritual in her dances. She looked for inspiration in mythologies from around the world, and created many exotic dances based on her idea of what she called "the Orient". Though these dances were immensely popular, they were far from authentic.

Pleats fan out to reinforce the shape of the dance

Court dance

SPECIAL DANCES, known as court dances, have been used throughout history to represent the ruling powers. All over the world, these ruling powers have made sumptuous and spectacular pageants a part of court life. These great spectacles displayed both their wealth and their control over vast numbers of people. Special court dances – regal and measured in their movements and performed on significant national occasions – reinforced the sense that a king is somehow different from his people and strengthened the position of a ruler. Court dances tend to be different from other dances. They are hierarchical, setting those at the source of power apart from the ordinary folk. Court dances have had far-reaching effects – they have given rise to the classical forms of dance in Europe, Asia, and Africa.

Bugaku performers are traditionally male, but are made-up to perform female roles

Kimonos used for bugaku are splendidly decorated

Mask represents Matsubara, a dragon king

Mask is made of wood, lacquer, and human hair

BUGAKU COURT DANCE
The bugaku and gagaku of Japan represent the world's oldest unbroken tradition of court dance and music. Some of today's performers claim they are 39th generation – that members of their family have performed dance and music throughout the last 1200 years! Some dances depict legendary battles, while others tell the story of meetings with supernatural beings and mythical beasts. The costume for bugaku often includes spectacular face masks.

Long, full kimonos are used for the more serious bugaku, which are known as "left" dances

A NATIONAL TREASURE
Bugaku is a dance of great dignity and stateliness, in which the performers move very slowly and elegantly through simple symmetrical patterns. For centuries, only the imperial household, government officials, and their guests were allowed to enjoy bugaku – the public could watch only after World War II. Today, these court dances are seen as reflecting qualities in the Japanese national character, and in 1995, bugaku and gagaku performers were proclaimed "living national treasures".

1ST OCTOBER PARADE, BEIJING, CHINA
In China, one of the major celebrations is the National Day festival on October 1st. This commemorates the day in 1949 that the Communist Party swept to power after years of revolution, and established the People's Republic of China. A love of pageantry and display is evident at festivals such as this, with colourful and perfectly synchronized fan dances, such as the one performed above.

The striking of stately poses is central to bugaku

COURT DANCE, GHANA
Carried by his courtiers, the elected king of the Asante in Ghana makes an impressive entrance. On special occasions, the king dances before his people to display his royal virtues. His dance movements are powerful but slow and dignified. The royal umbrella shading the king is also made to "dance" in time to the drums.

Asante finger rings, made of gold and encrusted with jewels

Golden Asante daggers

SUN EMBLEM
History remembers Louis XIV of France as *le roi soleil* – the Sun King. In 1653, aged 15, Louis performed as the rising sun in *Le ballet de la nuit*. In 1654, he performed as Apollo, the Greek sun god, in *Les noces de Pelée et de Thétis*. His costumes were liberally decorated with images of the sun.

ASANTE GOLD
Arab travellers in the 8th century described Ghana as "the land of gold", and for centuries gold has been the Asante people's emblem. Even today the king may dance while weighed down with masses of gold jewellery, and ornaments. In the past, the golden heads of heroic Asante kings decorated the royal throne, and a gold stool symbolized the unity of the nation.

Costume features emblems representing the sun

DANCE AT THE COURT OF LOUIS XIV
During his reign, Louis XIV drew the aristocracy to Versailles, his court outside Paris. The king was a well-known lover of dance; to be invited to dance in his presence was an honour that could launch a career, and Louis himself often performed. There was, however, an ulterior motive to Louis' court dances. By forcing the aristocrats to spend lavishly to keep up with his extravagance, while also keeping them away from their bases of power in the provinces, Louis kept them under his control financially and politically.

Louis XIV as the rising sun, *Le ballet de la nuit*, 1653

EUROPEAN COURT DANCE
In the 16th century, European princes competed with each other to have the most sumptuous court, emptying their treasuries to stage extravagant spectacles. In 1581, Catherine de' Medici and her son Henri III organized a royal wedding that included a series of court balls. These balls, held at the Louvre in Paris, were so lavish that they set the standard for all subsequent celebrations.

National heritage

The dragon king always includes the traditionally lucky colours of bright yellow or gold

PEOPLE DANCING TOGETHER share a sense of belonging. Dancing can remind them of their cultural identity and give them a sense of pride in their heritage. This experience can be particularly important in times of hardship, poverty, or oppression. When people find themselves powerless within their own country because it has been colonized, or when they have had to migrate because of economic difficulties or war, dance can return to them a sense of self-worth. Dance reinforces a sense of community and gives the outside world a positive image of a valuable heritage. Indeed, throughout history, there are examples of traditional dance being revived just as the first moves towards independence are made. Often this process polishes and standardizes the dances.

The dragon is formed of up to 12 sections. Each section is 1–3 m (3–9 ft) in length

DRAGON DANCE
In Chinese mythology, the heavenly dragon represents prowess, nobility, and good fortune. Traditionally the dragon dance was used to expel devils and bring people good luck. It was an essential part of many celebrations. Today it is especially associated with the Chinese New Year, and is performed throughout the world wherever large Chinese communities have settled. The dragon is followed by a noisy procession filled with drumming, fireworks and cheering crowds.

DANCING FOR INDEPENDENCE
Until the 19th century, the sardana of Catalonia, northeast Spain, was a simple dance, confined to a small area and performed by few people. As the Catalans unsuccessfully fought for independence from Spain, the dance spread and became a symbol of Catalan rebellion. During the 20th century, the fascist Franco government tried unsuccessfully to ban the sardana.

Several dancers, one drummer, and one leader are needed for the dragon dance

Chinese dragon dance

QUETZAL DANCE, MEXICO

In an effort to rediscover their pre-conquest identity, native Mexicans organized themselves into dance associations. At festivals and all-night vigils they perform traditional Aztec dances – some of which are named after Aztec gods, including the most powerful god of all, Quetzalcoatl.

Pheasant feathers

Quetzalcoatl, the fabulous Aztec plumed serpent-god of light

Headdress

Back of an Irish dance costume

ORISSI, EASTERN INDIA

The classical Indian dance orissi was at one time performed only by temple dancers called mahari. Like other classical forms, it was the subject of a cultural revival from 1930 to 1950, just as serious moves towards independence from Great Britain were being made.

Orissi dancer

Irish symbol of the shamrock

Green, white, and gold were favourite colours

Irish rose, hand-made in lace

Ute chief in tribal dress

IRISH DANCE AND IDENTITY

At the turn of the century, traditional Irish dance changed from an informal pastime into a symbol of nationalism. Dances were standardized and costumes became highly decorative. They were often adorned with Celtic designs copied from a 9th-century illuminated manuscript, the *Book of Kells*, which had just been discovered. Irish dance helped create an image of Irish nationhood.

Soft dance shoes

Kikuyu dancers performing a courtship dance

NATIVE AMERICAN POWWOW

White Americans frowned upon large inter-tribal gatherings, or powwows, because they felt threatened. In the 1930s, afraid of losing their cultural identity, Native Americans turned powwows into dance competitions, in which the dances of a glorious native past could be passed down to the younger generations.

Soft shoes allowed for intricate movements in dances, such as the slip jig

KIKUYU DANCERS, KENYA

In many East African societies young couples traditionally perform courtship dances. These dancers are performing such a dance for tourists, using adapted traditional movements.

Role reversal

WOMEN MAY DANCE AS MEN, and men as women, for a number of reasons. For example, in France in the late 19th century, ballet dancing had become a female activity and women took over the male roles. The male lead in *Coppélia* (1870) was choreographed for a ballerina called Eugénie Fiocre. In 17th- and 18th-century China and Japan, it was considered improper for women to go on stage, so certain male performers began to specialize in female roles. Role reversal is often thought of as humorous. All over the world, there are pantomimes featuring men dressed as women – the humour lies in the fact that the performers are obviously male and wear outrageous costumes. On the other hand, the Venda people of South Africa use role reversal in dance for a serious reason – it helps confuse evil spirits who might otherwise harm the dancers. Today in dance, the more common role reversal involves a male dancer playing a female role.

GROTESQUE FEMALE ROLES
In romantic ballet, female dancers represent the essence of beauty and elegance. There is a convention in ballet that such beauty cannot perform ugly roles, so these roles are performed by men dressed as women. In Frederick Ashton's *La fille mal gardée* (1960), Lise, the daughter of Widow Simone, loves Colas, but her mother is determined to marry her to Alain, the feeble-minded heir of a rich farmer. The ballet is full of slapstick and comic effects, both in the characters and in the choreography.

SALOME BY BÉJART
Only 10 lines are devoted to Salome in the Bible, yet her story has been portrayed and elaborated in all the arts, especially dance. Invited to dance at court in celebration of Herod's birthday, Salome pleased the king so much that she was allowed to ask for whatever she wanted. Her mother advised her to demand John the Baptist's head. Salome has usually been portrayed as a sensual woman, but the French choreographer Maurice Béjart wanted to break the stereotype of the female seductress and cast a man in the role.

Widow Simone, a caricature of a woman played by a man, here resembles a pantomime dame

CARABOSSE IN SLEEPING BEAUTY

The evil fairy Carabosse in *Sleeping Beauty* (1890), the Ugly Sisters in *Cinderella* (1948), and Widow Simone in *La fille mal gardée* (1960), are all comic or grotesque female roles played by men. In *Sleeping Beauty*, Carabosse places a curse on a baby princess. The curse is meant to kill her, but a good fairy, Lilac, changes it so that it makes the princess and her family sleep for 100 years.

Carabosse (right) in *Sleeping Beauty*

False hips

Crinoline

CARABOSSE'S COSTUME

The role of the reclusive Carabosse is traditionally danced by a man. As "the evil fairy" moves menacingly around the stage, her earthy, wicked nature is often depicted by a costume that enlarges her body with false hips and a crinoline. Over these, Carabosse wears a dress of dusty, ragged black.

SWAN LAKE, ADVENTURES IN MOTION PICTURES

Matthew Bourne's version of *Swan Lake*, choreographed for the company Adventures in Motion Pictures in 1995, stunned audiences. The ballet features no dainty ballerinas. Instead the swans are bare-chested men in feathery pantaloons, who convey both bird-like grace and a ferocity unknown in more traditional versions. They represent the assertive and masculine side of the male lead, Prince Siegfried, instead of the feminine grace and elegance of the lead ballerina, Odile/Odette.

KABUKI ONNAGATA

In many Japanese classical dance forms, only men were allowed to perform publicly. Since plays demanded female roles as well as male, some actors specialized in these. In the traditional dance form known as kabuki, these specialists are referred to as onnagata or woman-person. Elaborate make-up and costume help transform a mature man into a beautiful young woman, but the main transformation takes place in the gestures, bearing, and voice of the performer. Kabuki actors are trained not only to move like women on stage but also to think like women.

An onnagata headdress is often extremely ornate

Costumes can weigh up to 18 kg (40 lb) and are lavishly decorated

Kabuki kimonos are designed so they can be removed easily to transform the performer into another character

Something old, something new

From the time they were rediscovered, the painted and carved images of ancient Greek dancers have inspired modern dancers, including Isadora Duncan, who have enthused about their elegance.

DANCE LINKS THE PAST to the present. For dance to be properly appreciated, it needs to create images that are understood by its audience. If a dance is too remote, people will not be able to make sense of it. Dancers use the traditions of the past in various ways and for a number of reasons. Some reject all tradition because they feel it is not relevant to the present – they want to create dance that addresses contemporary issues. Others feel that they want to rediscover a golden, more meaningful past. Yet others see their work as the logical development of a thriving, existing tradition.

LOOKING FOR INSPIRATION

The American dancer Isadora Duncan (1878–1927) is the figure most noted for loosening the restrictions of ballet, which in her eyes, were unnatural and damaging. In her search for the real source of dance, she turned first to the art of classical Greece, second to nature, and third to herself. She once claimed her dance was "the art lost for two thousand years".

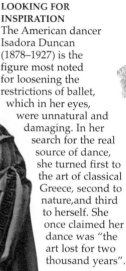

Duncan's clothing and costume were also inspired by ancient Greece

Motifs found on Greek friezes adorned the fabric of Duncan's costumes

Wildflowers are often embroidered in bright colours on folk costumes for both men and women

COPPELIA

In the ballet *Coppelia* (1870), a young man named Franz becomes so smitten with the charm of a mysterious girl that he forgets his fiancée Swanilda. The girl, however, is nothing but a doll. The dancers' costumes are inspired by a romantic idea of what central European peasantry might once have worn. Swanilda wears a blouse with puffed sleeves and an embroidered bodice over a wide skirt.

Garland of flowers on Swanilda's romantic tutu indicates that she is a village girl

FOLK DANCE IN BALLET

Many ballets incorporate elements of folk dance. In the first act of *Coppelia*, for example, the dancers perform a stylized version of the Polish dance mazurka. Traces of other European dances, like the Italian tarantella or the Hungarian czardas, have found their way into the ballet. This type of dancing is known as character dancing.

BUTOH EXPERIMENTAL DANCE, JAPAN

Butoh is Japan's best-known post-war experimental dance. With butoh, dancer and choreographer Hijikata Tatsumi (1928–1986) and his colleagues aimed to startle the Japanese into recognizing some of the unpleasant aspects of their society. They called their style of dancing ankoku butoh – the "dance of the dark soul". Even though butoh was a conscious attempt to break away from tradition, some elements remain rooted in classical dance. One of these elements is the very slow, stylized walk sometimes used in butoh, which can also be seen in noh.

Mask-like make-up resembles the controlled faces of the dance form kabaki

Shaved heads represent a rejection of the wigs of traditional dance

Rubbish bins and their lids provided percussion

Austere costumes are far removed from the elaborate kimonos of kabuki, noh, and bugaku

STOMPING FORWARDS IN TAP

In Britain in the late 1980s, some young dancers got together and founded a company called Tap Dogs. Rather than use conventional musical instruments as accompaniment, they explored the use of everyday and incongruous objects. The result was *Stomp,* an energetic and exhilarating work performed with great gusto.

Young men in magnificent costumes display fast and difficult footwork in the "fancy dance" contest of the powwow

A COMMON HERITAGE

Among Native Americans, two types of dance traditions co-exist. One is performed within individual tribal groups and fosters that group's identity. The other is performed by many tribal groups and fosters an overall Native American identity. Contemporary powwows (singing and dancing gatherings) feature a "fancy dance" contest.

Changes over time

THERE IS NO SINGLE HISTORY of dance; there are, rather, many histories of many dances around the world. However, all dances are rooted in the past, either because they embrace the traditions of the past, or they try to break away from them. We know of some dance traditions, such as those of ancient Greece, because the Greeks left clues in their paintings and sculptures. We know of other histories, such as how classical ballet developed, because teachers have left behind notes on steps or style. We can trace the history of western theatre dance back about 350 years, but other traditions, such as some of Japan's classical dance forms, go back some 1200 years. But even these dances are not unchanged relics – performers are always progressing and always innovating.

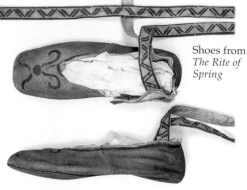

Shoes from *The Rite of Spring*

RITE OF SPRING
The Rite of Spring, a ballet about an adolescent girl dancing herself to death as a sacrifice to the god of spring, was first performed in Paris in 1913, and immediately caused a scandal. Stravinsky's discordant music and Nijinsky's ground-breaking choreography shocked an audience fed on conventional grace and beauty.

MARIE TAGLIONI
When the Italian star dancer Marie Taglioni (1804–1884) performed *La Sylphide* in 1832, she wore calf-length flowing costumes and pointe shoes to give the audience a full view of her flawless technique. Her success created such a demand for dancing en pointe that classical ballet was changed forever.

Female dancers are the stars of Fokine's Les Sylphides

A 17th-century ballet costume

Stiff bodice was difficult to move in

Longer skirt than modern costumes

LES SYLPHIDES
The popular one-act ballet *Les Sylphides* has only the barest of story lines: A poet is dazed by the presence of beautiful sylphs. With this work, first performed in 1909, the Russian choreographer Michel Fokine proved that ballet could survive and do well without being based on a complex dramatic situation.

COSTUME CHANGE
In 1760, the French choreographer Jean-George Noverre (1727–1810) wrote his *Lettres sur la danse et sur les ballets (Letters on Dancing)* as a reaction against the conventions that fettered French ballet. He appealed to dancers to take off their "enormous wigs and gigantic head-dresses which destroy the true proportion of the head with the body" and to discard the "stiff and cumbersome hoops which detract from the beauties of execution".

Costumes were sumptuous with gold and silver thread on silk

DIAGHILEV'S BALLETS RUSSES
Sergei Diaghilev's ballet company brought together the talents of the most modern dancers, designers, composers, and choreographers. From 1909 to 1929, it toured Europe and the US, and established ballet as a major theatre art.

Shorter tutu allowed classical ballerinas to show off their form and technique

A modern tutu

Rhinestone decoration glistens in the stage lights

MARIE CAMARGO
When the Belgian dancer Marie Camargo (1710–1770) first shortened her skirt to her ankles in 1726 to show off her entrechats (jumps in which the feet cross in the air before landing), she shocked traditionalists. Men's dance costume had always been designed to allow for leaps and spins, but it was not until the 19th century that all women dancers finally began wearing a lighter, less cumbersome costume – a tutu – that allowed greater freedom of movement.

MODERN BALLET AND DANCE
By the early 20th century, ballet was seen as restrictive and rigid, so choreographers simplified costumes and invented new movements. In 1992, American dancer and choreographer Twyla Tharp re-staged *Push Comes to Shove* (1976) for the Royal Ballet, with moves that were very different from the classical style.

An off-balance movement in Push Comes to Shove

Modern ballet footwork can look angular compared with classical ballet

Feet point outwards with heels together

First position

Feet are spaced

Second position

Erect torso with the spine acting as the centre

Third position

Legs turned out from the hips so body is open towards the front

Fourth position

Curved arms, held en haut, or high up

Fifth position

CENTURIES OF TRADITION AND TECHNIQUE
All dance traditions are grounded in technique. Dancers go through a progression of movements and exercises that create the ideal physique for each style. Ballet, for example, is based on five classical positions devised by Pierre Beauchamp (1631–1705) around 1700. The five positions lay down basic rules for ballet.

Groups and shapes

SOMETIMES THE RELATIONSHIP between dancers produces patterns that create specific dance formations. Group dances can be divided into two types. In the first, dancers keep their places within the formation throughout the dance: whether the dancers move in a circle, in straight lines, in figures of eight, or in spirals, they remain in line and are led by the dance leader. In the second type, dancers change places through movements, including chains, crossings, bridges, or stars. They dance independently within a dance, but interact with other dancers at different times. Each dancer usually ends up back in his or her starting position.

KOREAN FAN DANCERS
Dancers can carry props to create beautiful and colourful shapes in the air. For example, some traditional Korean dancers use large fans to extend their movements. Grouped together, the shapes and movements of the fan dancers create a stunning spectacle.

SQUARE DANCING
Modern square dancing is largely derived from a 19th-century European dance known as the quadrille, where four couples danced in a square formation. In the modern square dance, couples may change partners, or exchange places, or take turns dancing alone. The figures can be quite complex and a "caller" shouts out instructions.

In many dances, male dancers hold each other's hands or a handkerchief

The dance leader often performs his own improvized steps

The traditional skirt is known as a foustanella

GREEK DANCING
Many dances in Greece are performed in open circles: the dancers form a chain, holding each other by the hands, waists, or shoulders and move in a circle. The first and last positions are clearly distinguished. The leader can take the chain wherever he or she wants. The order taken by the dancers usually reflect's seniority. Commonly, men are at the beginning of a chain in descending order of age, followed by women, also ranked according to age.

In Hindu mythology, the gods create the universe by dancing in a magnificent circular formation, kicking away the dust of chaos as they go

IN THE ROUND

The circle is a very common dance formation. It can move either clockwise or anticlockwise. Any central figures in a circle may have special significance. All the dancers in a circle are usually on equal terms with one another – everyone can see everyone else. If the dancers hold one another, they have to move in unison.

FORMATIONS IN MUSICALS

American musicals developed the Eastern European folk tradition of the double storey, in which dancers of one circle would stand or sit on the shoulders of another circle. The musicals of the 1920s and 1930s achieved stunning visual effects based on the multiple storey.

Krishna is often represented as a heavenly dancer

Flower detail on border of muslin cloth echoes the pattern of the dance

MAYPOLES AROUND THE WORLD

The centre of a circle is the focus of a circular dance. Maypole dances, in which participants dance around a long pole, exist everywhere. The pole often symbolizes fertility.

Bolivian tape dance

Ribbons held by the dancer are twisted attractively one over another in the course of the dance

An 18th-century embroidered muslin cloth showing Krishna dancing with the gopis (milkmaids), North India

Dance and community

WHETHER WE ARE watching or participating, dance is a way of uniting communities, and is commonly linked to leisure, sport, and competition. Ballroom dancing is now one of the most popular recreations in Europe. Its beauty and romance allow both the dancers and an audience to escape reality. Meanwhile, in dancehalls throughout the world, young people meet and let off steam on the dancefloor. Carnivals – including the spectacular annual events of Rio de Janeiro and New Orleans – provide ample opportunity for entertainment and merry-making, while in many areas, folk dances preserve the traditions of the past, while giving a sense of wellbeing to the participants.

Female dancers wear exquisite gowns, often embroidered with Austrian rhinestones

Partners make imperceptible signals with their index fingers to indicate changes in rhythm or steps

For certain dances such as the waltz, male dancers dress formally in white tie and tails

BALLROOM DANCING
In hundreds of clubs in the UK and throughout Europe, thousands of people attend ballroom-dancing classes in order to learn the skills necessary to attend tea dances and enter competitions. Ballroom dancing was popularized by Irene and Vernon Castle in the US in the 1910s. Today, fans of the waltz, fox trot, cha-cha, and quickstep feel that this sophisticated style of dancing, with its melodic accompaniment and beautiful costumes, is reminiscent of an earlier, more elegant time.

Feathers enhance the dancer's graceful movements

ORIGINS OF BALLROOM DANCE
Contemporary ballroom dancing grew out of several traditions. Regional dances performed by the common people were the basis for many of these dances. In the 16th century, travelling dance masters began teaching both "city" and "country" styles of dance to their pupils, and the two styles influenced each other. By the 19th century, this style of dance was further enriched by the inclusion of African influences.

CARNIVAL
Both in Europe and in the Americas, carnivals have allowed people to dance in the streets, and generally turn the social order upside down. For this reason, the authorities have often frowned upon carnival merry-making

FOLK DANCE
The Industrial Revolution in Europe inspired nostalgia for an idealized golden past – a time when peasants enjoyed traditional country pursuits. This interest in the life of the common country people widened to include dance, and in 1893 a Folk Dance Society was set up in Stockholm, Sweden. Many more such societies followed in other parts of Europe in an attempt to rescue vanishing folk cultures.

Swedish folk dancers in traditional dress

1992 Winter Olympic Games opening ceremony, Albertville, France

Bold movements and vivid costumes could be seen from a distance

DANCE AND CEREMONY
Throughout history, as rituals and ceremonies became meaningless or were lost, they were replaced by new ones. In modern times, sport is one of the last remaining – and most important – pursuits that people enjoy together. Pageantry and ritual surround major sporting events. The Winter Olympic Games are watched by people all over the world. The spectacular opening and closing ceremonies are always marked by presentational dance and pageant.

Paris dancehall, France, late 19th century

EARLY DANCEHALLS
Ordinary people were generally excluded from the elegant balls held by the aristocracy. By the late 18th century, they began to establish public dancehalls of their own for the enjoyment of dancing. By the 1890s, people in large cities were flocking to halls, such as the one shown here, to dance and have a good time.

Sets for dance

DANCE CAN BE PERFORMED in all sorts of surroundings, from the most elaborate theatre stage to a clearing in the bush. The place where the dance is performed is known as the set. A set has a great influence on the relationship between dancers and audience. Its appearance is dictated by the location and the type of dance. For example, a processional street dance must have a mobile set, if it has one at all. Western theatres tend to have more lavish sets, while oriental theatres (with the exception of the complex sets often used for Japanese kabuki) tend to have fixed, plain backgrounds. If there is no set, performers must bring a story to life by means of their bodies alone, making the audience "see" the voyages, hunts, or battles taking place.

DANCING IN THE STREET
Street parades, such as this festival in Japan, invite a community to take over public spaces and celebrate in dance. Open-air dance is more appropriate to audience participation than theatre performances.

SET DESIGN FOR SWAN LAKE, 1989
Set is all-important in establishing the mood of a ballet. This model is for the ballroom in Act III of *Swan Lake,* one of the most famous and popular classical ballets of all time. With its score by the 19th-century Russian composer Peter Ilyich Tchaikovsky, the set was designed to evoke a regal atmosphere by placing *Swan Lake* in the court of the Russian tsar. The set features fantasy elements combined with accurate historical details. The jewels, heavy loops of gold, and imperial purple drapes all convey the magnificence of the tsar's palaces.

Original sketch for the 1943 set

UPDATING SET DESIGNS FOR SWAN LAKE, 1943
The Royal Ballet in the UK performed *Swan Lake* to audiences of thousands against a set that was first designed in 1943. The old set and costumes were updated in 1989, giving a different look to one of the world's favourite ballets and creating a different atmosphere for new generations of ballet-goers. The production, costumes, and sets were all transformed by designer Yolande Sonnabend.

Set model for production of *Swan Lake* at the Royal Opera House, London, UK, 1989

GOING TO A DISCO
Discotheques – nightclubs where people danced primarily to recorded music (rather than live) – were introduced in the 1950s but were most popular in the late 1970s and 1980s. Large clubs were filled with crowds, and featured lasers and light shows to create a fantastic environment. Record companies helped discos become more popular by releasing disco singles and generating big money for the entertainment industry.

SWAN LAKE, **ACT III**
The ballroom scene, shown here, is at the centre of *Swan Lake*. During the ball, Prince Siegfried is deceived into proposing marriage to Odile, the daughter of the evil sorceror, Rothbart. Rothbart watches gleefully as the pair dance a glorious pas de deux.

The queen's throne

Lady-in-waiting

The evil sorceror Rothbart

Prince Siegfried's mother, the queen

Sketch looks menacing

Puttin' on the Ritz, set design, 1929

Movements make the actual set less menacing

Puttin' on the Ritz actual set, 1929

DANCE SETS AND HOLLYWOOD
Some of the most amazing dance sets ever seen were created for 1920s Hollywood musicals such as *Puttin' on the Ritz* by Busby Berkerley (1895 – 1976). Having introduced sound to the movies in 1927, producers fed the cinema-going public song-and-dance extravaganzas as a vehicle for the new technology. The spectacular sets successfully held the audience's attention despite sometimes weak plots and scripts! Berkerley was a master at lavish musicals – even today, the dance settings in his movies seem fantastically imaginative.

Ornamental details evoke a sense of fantasy

Bejewelled set was inspired by the Russian court jewellers, Fabergé

Queen's throne

SHOE MISTRESS OR MASTER
Dancers often wear special shoes, like pointe shoes, which are specifically designed for their type of dancing. A shoe mistress or master needs to look after the shoes, making sure that they look good, that they are the right colour for the costumes, and that they are replaced when necessary.

Scale model for The Nutcracker

STAGE SETS
To create the set – the scenery on the stage – the designer discusses the overall vision with the choreographer before designing the set on paper. When these ideas are approved, an accurate scale model is usually built to see if the design works in three dimensions. When built, the design may be altered until the artistic director feels it is just right.

Behind the scenes

WHEN WE THINK ABOUT theatre dance we think first of dancers, then of choreographers, then – possibly – of composers, musicians, and designers. Many more people, however, are involved behind the scenes in dance productions. Dance is full of non-dancers: notators who write down steps and restage works; lighting designers who transform moods and enrich the sets; teachers and therapists who keep dancers' bodies finely tuned; people who look after shoes, costumes, and wigs; sound technicians, stagehands, painters, carpenters, box office personnel, front-of-house managers, public relations people, administrators, critics...the list is endless! Most of these people never make a dance movement or are even seen by an audience. Nonetheless, they are an integral part of dance, and no performance can take place without their input. Dance productions are a cooperative venture, both on and off the stage.

Paints and paintbrush

Painting the set for
Alice in Wonderland,
1995

Massive flowers give a fanciful, fairytale impression

Lighting rig

LIGHTING
Stage lights can create a huge variety of moods and impressions, and enhance the theatre sets and dance costumes. In the ballet *Petrushka*, for example, blue lights are used to give the cold feeling of a Russian winter. Lights hung above the stage and in the auditorium are referred to as the rig. The rig is controlled electronically from a central box.

PAINTERS AND CARPENTERS
Once the sets are designed, they have to be made to create the impression presented on paper. Background scenes may be painted on to backdrops. Alternatively, they may be built out of wood, with windows and doors through which dancers can enter and leave the stage. The sets need to be maintained as they are moved in and out of the theatre and taken on tour.

Small scissors are used to cut thread

Pins are used to hold fabric together before sewing

A pair of small needlework scissors and pins

A dressmaker in her studio

WARMING UP

Prior to a performance, dancers need to warm up onstage at a portable barre brought in by stagehands. They may do the first part of a class, starting with pliés or kneebends, or they may have their own exercise routines. The warm up gradually builds up to include strenuous exercises involving the feet, ankles, and knees. Good warm up is crucial to dancers to stop them from injuring their muscles. Dancers wear a variety of casual, comfortable clothing to keep them warm before getting into their costumes.

MAKING COSTUMES

Costume designers make detailed sketches of their ideas and often attach samples of possible fabrics. These are given to skilled dressmakers and tailors who then turn the designs into reality. Costumes must never restrict movements. Sleeves must allow the arms to move freely, and fastenings must be comfortable for the dancer, but also allow for quick changes. Costumiers, as they are sometimes called, can become close to the dancers they dress. Anna Pavlova's personal dresser, Manya Charchevenikova, stayed with the great dancer until her death, becoming an intimate and privileged friend.

Make-up brushes and lipstick

MAKING UP

Make-up is used to accentuate a dancer's features. It must be quite vivid and applied heavily so that dancers' faces can be seen under strong stage lighting. Different make-up can create different expressions, like mournfulness or fierceness. Sometimes it can completely change the shape of a dancer's face, especially if "putty" is used to make false noses and chins. Make-up for beautiful characters such as the Sugar Plum Fairy in *The Nutcracker* concentrates on eyes and lips.

Specially lit mirror is needed to ensure make-up can be seen under lights

Making up for *The Nutcracker*

Warming up at a portable barre

Famous dancers

A DANCE EXISTS ONLY while it is being performed – and yet sometimes a performance can leave an impression so strong that it stays in the memory forever. Some dancers dazzle an audience with their technical skill and physical prowess, while others stir us emotionally, through their special ability to interpret a story. Few dancers are capable of both in equal measure, but those who are often become so famous that their names go down in history. In fact, dance history is largely the history of the most famous dancers – unique performers and teachers who devoted their lives to dance, such as Anna Pavlova, Vaslav Nijinsky, and Rukmini Devi. In the eyes of the world, their names are legendary and have come to symbolize the dance they loved so much.

RUKMINI DEVI
Fired by the magic of Pavlova, Rukmini Devi (1904–1986) dedicated her life to the revival of classical dance in her native India, enchanting audiences by her performances.

Pavlova's main talent lay in her expressive movements

Pavlova as a bacchante (a dancing girl from Greek mythology)

KATHERINE DUNHAM
An exceptionally skilled and admired dancer, choreographer, and scholar, Katherine Dunham (b.1910) created a completely original dance technique in the late 1930s. She combined ballet with movements from African and Caribbean dance traditions. Dunham is often seen as a major figure in African-American dance, but in fact her pioneering technique is very much part of mainstream modern dance.

Katherine Dunham, who founded her own dance school in 1945

Rogers and Astaire in Roberta (1935)

FRED ASTAIRE AND GINGER ROGERS
A film producer once told dancer Fred Astaire (1899–1987) that he could only "dance a little." Astaire, with dance partner Ginger Rogers (1911–1995), later became an international star. Gracefully anticipating each other's smallest movements, the pair expressed perfectly the romance of ballroom dancing.

ANNA PAVLOVA
To the thousands who saw her perform – and the millions who know her name – the Russian ballerina Anna Pavlova (1881–1931) was the essence of ballet. An outstandingly expressive performer, she was famous for her ability to interpret a story. Pavlova once said that she wanted to "dance for everybody in the world," and she toured constantly. From 1910 to 1925, she visited Europe, the Americas, Asia, and South Africa, performing nearly 4,000 times and inspiring many dancers and choreographers.

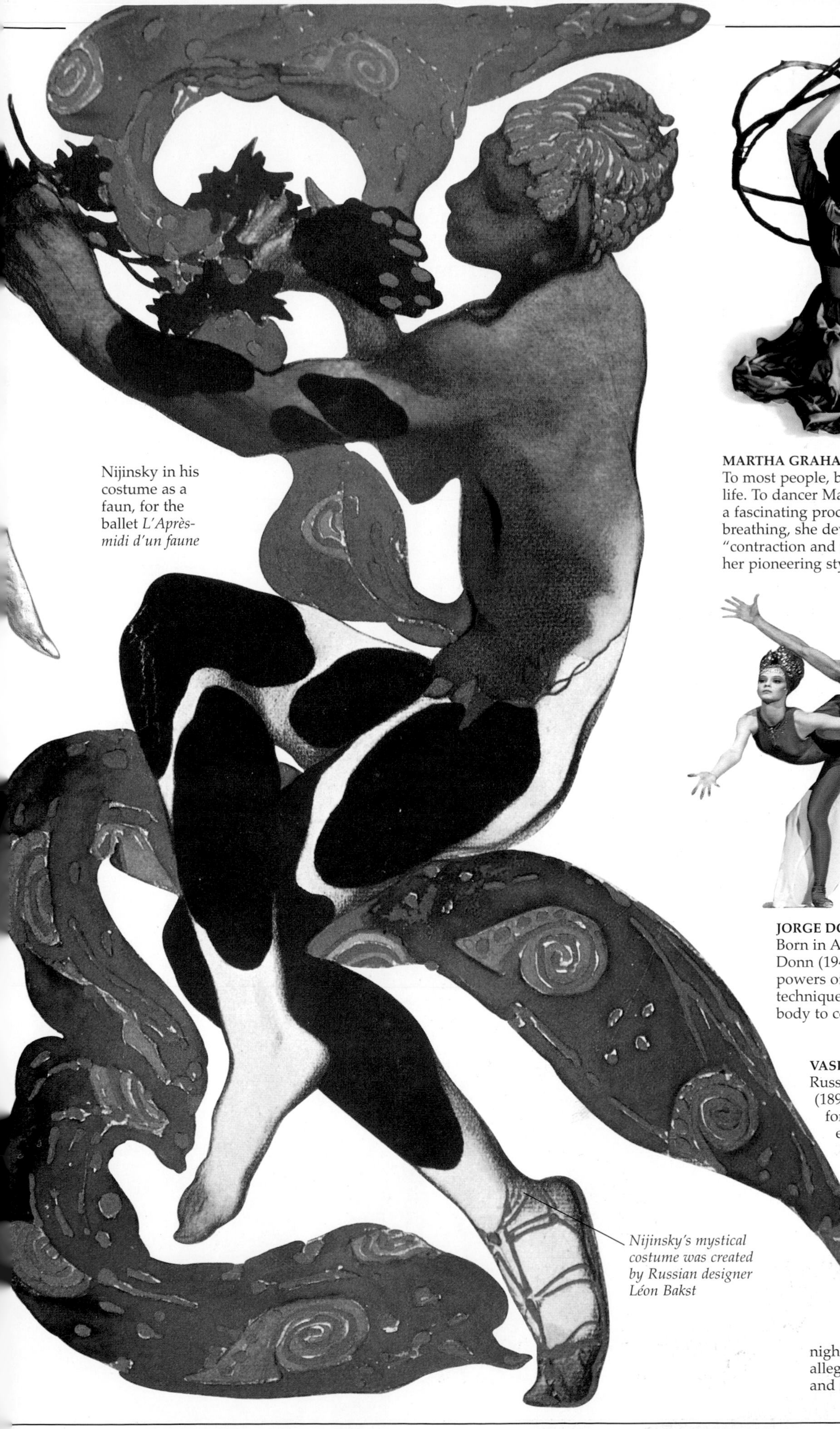

Nijinsky in his
costume as a
faun, for the
ballet *L'Après-
midi d'un faune*

*Nijinsky's mystical
costume was created
by Russian designer
Léon Bakst*

Martha Graham
in *Salem Shore*
(1941)

MARTHA GRAHAM

To most people, breathing is a mundane fact of
life. To dancer Martha Graham (1894–1991), it was
a fascinating process. From her observations of
breathing, she developed the principles of
"contraction and release," on which she based
her pioneering style of modern dance.

JORGE DONN

Born in Argentina, ballet dancer Jorge
Donn (1947–1992) was famous for his
powers of interpretation. His flawless
technique enabled him to use his whole
body to communicate with an audience.

VASLAV NIJINSKY

Russian dance legend Vaslav Nijinsky
(1890–1950) is best remembered
for his remarkable jumps, or
elevations. In the 1911 ballet *Le
Spectre de la Rose*, in which he
portrayed the spirit of a rose,
he soared out of a window
into the night, creating
probably the most
famous leap in ballet
history. Nijinsky was
also famous for
his controversial
choreographies, such
as *L'Après-midi d'un
faune* (1912). On its opening
night, members of the audience
alleged that this ballet was obscene,
and fights broke out.

Choreography

THE WORD CHOREOGRAPHY comes from the Greek "graphia", meaning "to write down", and "choros", meaning "dance". Today, choreography refers more to the invention of dances than to the mere writing down of dance steps, and a choreographer is an inventor of a new sequence of dance steps. The importance of the choreographer varies from one society to another. In Japan, some classical dances have been choreographed and are performed only by specific families. In many African and European folk dances, some dance steps are remembered and handed down through generations – they may be named after their choreographers. In western theatre dance like ballet, choreography is a profession and choreographers can become world famous.

Perrot with Carlotta Grisi, for whom he choreographed *Giselle* (1841)

JULES PERROT
During his lifetime, Jules Perrot (1810–1894) created expressive choreography that helped tell the story of his ballets through movement. His convincing characters came from all social classes, but his heroes were frequently of humble origins.

MARIE RAMBERT
Trained in a method of rhythmic analysis known as eurythmics, Polish-born Marie Rambert (1888–1982) studied in Paris. While there, she was hired by Sergei Diaghilev of the Ballets Russes to help dancers with the complex score of the ballet, *The Rite of Spring*. In 1931, she established Britain's first permanent ballet company and school in London, and nurtured the talents of famous choreographers, including Frederick Ashton.

Lean, long-legged dancers were ideal for Balanchine's type of work

GEORGE BALANCHINE
The name of George Balanchine (1904–1983) is synonymous with American classical ballet. Originally from Russia, Balanchine emigrated to the US and set up the School of American Ballet in 1934, planting the seed for the future New York City Ballet (1948). Balanchine's swift, athletic style came to be seen as distinctively American.

Balanchine (centre) demonstrating a pas de deux position, 1950

MERCE CUNNINGHAM

After working with Martha Graham, the American dancer Merce Cunningham (born 1919) developed his own original style. Although he worked out his dance movements in some detail, their order was left up to the performers – or even determined by flipping a coin! In his choreographies, he gives equal importance to each area of the stage and sees sound, decor, and movement as independent entities.

The position of this dancer is recorded in Benesh Movement Notation (BMN), below right

Hands are held above the head

In BMN, five horizontal lines represent the level of the head, shoulders, waist, knees, and floor

Elbows and knees are indicated by crossing basic signs

	Head
	Shoulder
	Waist
	Knees

Floor

des Vaisseaux 41

Musical score is included to ensure that music and steps complement each other

Step symbols are placed beside a central line

Right and left are shown by placement of symbols on either side of the central line

Feuillet's notation system

BENESH MOVEMENT NOTATION

Benesh movement notation, or BMN, was developed in England in the 1940s by Rudolf and Joan Benesh. It is a movement – rather than dance – notation, and can record what the body does in any activity, whether it is ballet or football. Today many dance companies employ Benesh notators to write down scores of the choreographies in their repertoire.

NOTATION SYSTEM

In 1701, a French dancing master, Raoul Feuillet (1675–1730), wrote his *Chorégraphie ou l'art d'écrire la danse (Choreography or the Art of Writing Dance)*, giving a notation system for writing down basic movements, rather than the conventional steps that everyone knew. The system quickly became accepted by dance masters throughout Europe. It allowed them to recreate each other's choreographies with a minimum of effort.

Central line shows the floor pattern of the dance

Left hand is in front of the body with palm facing front

Right foot is raised to waist level behind the body

Right arm is raised to shoulder level behind the body

Position of body in BMN

Left foot is on pointe

ARABESQUE IN BMN

This arabesque is notated as a static picture. A full score would indicate how the dancer moves into and out of the position as well as her timing. The left arm is raised in front of the body (vertical dash) above the head, the right arm is behind (a dot) at shoulder level. The left foot is en pointe, level with the body (horizontal dash), while the right foot is raised behind the body.

Dance crazes

DANCING IS A PART of every society's culture – and a dance craze can test a society's tolerance levels. The history of dance in Europe and the US shows how some dances that today represent elegance and sophistication were once thought deeply shocking. For example, when the waltz was introduced, polite society was appalled because for the first time men and women danced in a close embrace, instead of at arm's length. Some dances were deemed so outrageous that they were outlawed. In the 1910s, one woman spent 50 days in jail for dancing a banned dance called the turkey trot! Despite such reactions, fashionable people through the ages have wanted to learn the latest crazes.

SHOCKING WALTZ
In the 1780s, the waltz gripped Germany. At first, people frowned upon the abandonment of the whirling couples, and claimed that the dance was weakening the bodies and minds of the younger generation.

DOING THE CAKEWALK
The cakewalk was a craze of the 1890s. The dance originated on sugar-cane plantations, where, after harvest, plantation owners would set up a dance competition for their enslaved African workers. The slaves who made up the fanciest dance steps won cakes. The cakewalk, with its strut-like steps, broke the tradition of smooth gliding dances that had been dominant in the past.

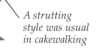

A strutting style was usual in cakewalking

CHARLESTON
In the 1920s, the charleston conquered New York. Its origins dated back to World War I, when many African-Americans left the poverty of the southern states to work in New York's munitions factories. They brought with them a high-stepping dance style, which was featured in popular African-American musicals, such as *Runnin' Wild*. From the shows, the craze spread all over the city and to all sections of society.

Sometimes dancers knocked hats off the heads of their audience with their spectacular high kicks

Can can dancers lifted and swirled the fronts of their dresses

The can can's finale eventually featured splits

A poster by Toulouse-Lautrec showing "Le Moulin Rouge"

CAN CAN AT THE MOULIN ROUGE
In the 1830s, the can can, featuring a line of high-kicking women, hit Parisian ballrooms. As the can can became more wild and acrobatic, it was seen as immoral. By the 1880s, it had moved into music halls, such as "Le Moulin Rouge". The French artist Henri de Toulouse-Lautrec (1864–1901) immortalized the dance in his posters.

ROCK 'N' ROLL DANCERS

In the 1950s, rock 'n' roll music and dance were all the rage. Couples moved exuberantly around the dance floor, reinventing old steps from the Charleston and the lindy hop (a fast, improvized 1930s dance). Partners showed off to friends with acrobatic moves, such as "air steps", in which the man spun his partner through the air.

In rock 'n' roll dancing, the man leads his partner through different moves

Chubby Checker, who had a hit single called "The Twist"

LET'S TWIST AGAIN

The twist caught on in the 1960s. It brought a development as revolutionary as the first closed-couple waltz – partners let go of each other! They stepped apart to wriggle and shake on their own. No one led, no one followed, no one even needed to know the steps!

The leading dancer always holds his partner's right hand with his own left hand

Light-up heels

Adapter for recharging batteries in shoes

discoshoes

Dancers try to make even difficult moves look effortless

DISCO MANIA

Dancers have always invented dramatic outfits: red boots for tango, beaded fringed dresses for the Charleston – even sandals with flashing lights for disco. These "disco shoes", complete with batteries, became fashionable after the movie *Saturday Night Fever* was released in 1977, and disco became the hottest dance craze of its time

Did you know?

FASCINATING FACTS

Rock art found in southern Africa shows prehistoric dancers. The paintings were made by the San people over a period of around 10,000 years. San shamen took part in trance-like dances performed to harness the energies of the spirit world.

Prehistoric rock art of San dancers

The leotard is named after its inventor Jules Léotard, a French acrobat who performed the first flying trapeze act on 12 November 1859. He wore a tight-fitting outfit to show off his muscles!

Dance star Joaquín Cortés was born in Cordoba, Spain, in 1969 and joined the Spanish National Ballet at 15. In 1992, he formed the Joaquín Cortés Flamenco Ballet. His *Pasión Gitana* (*Gipsy Passion*) has been enjoyed by more than a million people around the world.

Spanish-born Joaquín Cortés in performance

The youngest ballerinas ever to play leading roles were the "Baby Ballerinas" who joined the Ballets Russes in 1933 – Irina Baronova was just 13, Tamara Toumanova was 14, and Tatiana Riabouchinska was 15. The girls starred in ballets choreographed by the great George Balanchine.

Florenz Ziegfeld was the creator of the *Ziegfeld Follies*, a revue show that ran on Broadway from 1907 to 1931. The *Follies* featured comic sketches, songs, and dance routines from the longest ever chorus line. A film based on the show, directed by Vincent Minnelli, came out in 1946.

Each spring, the Cherry Blossom Dance is performed by novice geishas in the Japanese city of Kyoto. The girls dance on a stage strewn with pink and white cherry blossom to the accompaniment of traditional instruments, such as the banjo-like shamisen.

The Dance of the Seven Veils is based on the journey of a Mesopotamian goddess to the underworld. At each of the seven gates, Istar had to take off one of her powers; in the dance, the performer sheds the seven veils that cover her body.

In ancient Greek mythology, the Nine Muses were patron goddesses, each associated with one of the arts. Terpsichore was the Muse associated with dancing.

Nureyev plays Romeo to Fonteyn's Juliet

The most curtain calls for a ballet was 89, after Rudolf Nureyev and Margot Fonteyn danced in *Swan Lake* in Vienna, Austria, in 1964. The duo also delighted audiences in *Romeo and Juliet*, *Giselle*, *Marguerite and Armand*, and *Les Sylphides*.

Some pop songs have their own dance. Michael Jackson created the "moonwalk" for his hit *Thriller* in 1982, while Madonna caused a stir with the "vogue" in 1990.

Michael Jackson's *Thriller*

Inhabitants of the Faeroe Islands in the Atlantic Ocean perform circle dances. The Faeroese are descendants of Norwegian Vikings. They dance in time to sung ballads that tell of young heroes who defeat trolls, dwarfs, and giants.

The most popular ballet is Tchaikovsky's *The Nutcracker*, which was first performed in 1892. The ballet was based on a fantastical tale by German writer Ernst Hoffmann, and includes the famous Dance of the Sugar Plum Fairy. Tchaikovsky wrote the music to two other great ballets: *Swan Lake* and *The Sleeping Beauty*.

QUESTIONS AND ANSWERS

An old engraving of a Lipizzaner

Q Which horses are trained to dance?

A Lipizzaner stallions dance at the Spanish Riding School in Vienna, Austria. The finale of a Lipizzaner display is often the Grand Quadrille, a dance that involves up to eight horses (and riders), all in step. Lipizzaners were also used in 2002 by the American choreographer Paula Josa-Jones. Her piece, *Ride*, featured six horses and riders, along with seven modern dancers.

Linedancers

Q What is the most popular dance in the world today?

A Improvized disco moves are more popular than any set steps. However, around the world there are thousands of clubs devoted to linedancing, and millions of dancers. Linedances are American folk dances, where the dancers are always in rows, and move from back to front in a square formation.

A perfomance of *Riverdance*, starring Michael Flatley

Q Who turned Carmen into a car mechanic?

A Carmen is the passionate gypsy heroine from the opera *Carmen*, written by 19th-century French composer Georges Bizet, and first performed in Paris, France, in 1875. In the dramatic finale, Carmen is killed by a jealous lover. British choreographer and director Matthew Bourne created a new ballet, *The Car Man* (2000), based on the opera. Famous for his gender-bending *Swan Lake* (see p.41), Bourne cast a male dancer in the "Carmen" role. Luca is a handsome drifter who takes a job as a car mechanic at Dino's Garage. However, just like Carmen, Luca's magnetic good looks soon provoke jealousy – and dark tragedy.

Q Which is the longest-running musical?

A Andrew Lloyd Webber's *Cats* closed on Broadway in 2000 after nearly 18 years of sellout performances. The musical was also the longest-running in London's West End. *Cats* is based on *The Old Possum's Book of Practical Cats*, a collection of poems by TS Eliot. Feline characters including Old Deuteronomy, Grizabella, and Mister Mistoffelees all performed their own songs and dances.

Q Who was the world's most highly paid dancer?

A Michael Flatley entered the record books in 1999 as the world's highest paid dancer, earning £1 million a week. His legs were insured for £25 million. Chicago-born Flatley made his name in 1994 with *Riverdance*, an Irish dance routine for the Eurovision Song Contest. The following year this was turned into a full-length show. His *Lord of the Dance* (1996) and *Feet of Flames* (1998) have also been enjoyed by millions worldwide.

Matthew Bourne's *The Car Man*, a modern reworking of *Carmen*

Record Breakers

🌼 **BIGGEST DANCE**
Around 72,000 people gathered to do the chicken dance at a fair in Ohio, USA, in 1996.

🌼 **BIGGEST TAP DANCE**
The biggest tap dance involved 6,952 dancers and was held in Stuttgart, Germany, in 1998.

🌼 **FASTEST TAP DANCER**
At his fastest, Irish dancer Michael Donnellan can make 40 taps a second!

🌼 **MOST TURNS IN A BALLET**
Ballerina Pierina Legnani performed 32 fouettes (furiously fast turns on one foot) as Odile/Odette in *Swan Lake*. Ever since, everyone playing that role has had to try and do the same.

🌼 **FURTHEST DANCE**
In 1996 David Meenan tap danced a distance of over 37 km (23 miles).

🌼 **LONGEST CONGA**
Nearly 120,000 people joined in the conga in Miami, USA, on 13 March 1988.

World of dance

THE TRADITIONAL DANCES performed by peoples around the world are different types of folk dancing. Some of these date back thousands of years; others have arisen recently, to give expression to new experiences. Energetic or soulful, sacred or even political, all these dances bring people together.

An Indian classical dancer

AUSTRALIA & OCEANIA

Australian Aborigines and New Zealand Maoris have kept alive traditional dances. So have the peoples from other South Sea islands, such as Hawaii and Tahiti.

Hawaiian dancers

HULA DANCING
"Hula kahiko", or ancient hula, used dance and chanting to retell Hawaii's history. The dance has its roots in ancient rituals performed by men to thank the gods. Today, "hula auwana", or modern hula, is also performed – simply to express happiness.

NORTH AMERICA

Native Americans have their own dances, such as the drum dances performed by Canadian Inuit. With white settlers, came folk dances from Europe. In the 20th century, America led the way in popular dances, from jazz dancing to rock 'n' roll and disco.

STREET STYLE
In 1969 artist Afrika Bambaataa encouraged youths from poor areas of New York in the USA to start the first breakdancing crews. With a portable stereo (ghetto-blaster) playing hip-hop music as accompaniment, the kids danced acrobatically.

Breakdancing in New York City

SOUTH & CENTRAL AMERICA

A conchero dancer

The oldest dances in South and Central America are those of Native Indian peoples. However, there is also a rich heritage from Europe, especially Spain, as seen in ballroom dances such as the tango. African influences came through the black slaves who had been taken to South America to work. Their influence gave rise to dances such as the samba.

A Mardi Gras dancer, Brazil

CONCHERO DANCER
Mexican concheros are Native Indians who perform at fiestas. Their dances date back to around the time of the Spanish Conquest. The dancers wear tall, plumed headdresses, showing the influence of their Mixtec and Aztec heritage. They are accompanied by rhythmic, hypnotic drumming.

MARDI GRAS
The world's biggest dance festival is held each year in Rio de Janeiro, Brazil, to mark the beginning of the Christian period of fasting, Lent. For five days, "schools" of costumed dancers parade the streets.

EUROPE

Dances of Europe include the waltz, polka, and flamenco. Many are "couple dances", for a man and woman. Europe is also the birthplace of ballet, which originated in France in the 17th century.

Danish children folk dancing

DANISH DANCE
Every year in Denmark, there are two big festivals of folk music and dance: one at Skagen in June and the other at Tønder in August. Dances include the fast-moving pols, which was popular in the 1600s.

PORTUGUESE FADO
The fado is an undulating, multicultural dance. The dance itself comes from the rhythmic traditions of Africans and Brazilians living in 19th-century Lisbon, Portugal. But the accompaniments are Portuguese guitar and traditional, sung ballads.

A fado dancer takes a rest

From the painting *O Fado* (1910) by José Malhoa

AFRICA

African dances are often performed for a function: to prepare for war, give thanks, or mark the stages in people's lives. In West Africa, dancers often wear sculpted masks.

Swazi men dance during the incwala

INCWALA
Incwala is the name of a five-day harvest festival held in Swaziland, southern Africa. On the third day, the king performs a sacred dance to please his Swazi ancestors, then he eats the first pumpkin of the harvest. After the king tosses away the rind, his people sing and dance, before feasting on the "first fruits" of the year.

ASIA

Asia is the world's largest continent. It is also home to a wide variety of dance traditions, such as the bellydances of the Middle East, classical dances of India, and the elaborate, theatrical court dances of China, Japan, and Korea.

THAI DANCE
In Thailand, traditional temple dancers wear intricate, gilded costumes. Their dance is a form of prayer and meditation. Every movement is elegant, precise, and controlled.

A Thai dancer kneels at Erawan Shrine, Bangkok

A Chinese dragon welcomes in the New Year in Hong Kong

CHINESE NEW YEAR
To celebrate the New Year, Chinese people gather in the streets to watch dancing lions and dragons. Inside each costume, there may be 50 dancers or more. The dragon is associated with long life and prosperity.

Find out more

IF YOU ARE NOW A DANCE FAN, here are some ways that you can find out more about it. You will be able to see artists performing by visiting the theatre or even by watching the television – dance is an important part of many films, especially romantic old musicals. Many theatres also give behind-the-scenes tours, so that you can see sets at close hand. Visit your library for books about famous dancers or the history of dance. You can also study dance at some schools and colleges. Best of all, attend a dance class – whether you go for ballet, tap, or salsa, it is sure to be fun.

USEFUL WEBSITES

- A ballet website with news, interviews, and profiles
  www.ballet.co.uk
- Fort Worth Dallas Ballet website with a great section for children
  www.fwdballet.com
- Specialist website dedicated to Indian classical dance
  www.tarang-classical-indian-music.com
- Teen site covering all aspects of dance
  www.young-dancers.org
- Specialist folk dancing website
  www.folkdancing.org

Julie Diana and Yuri Possokhov in *The Sandpaper Ballet*

DANCE THERAPY
Dance has the power to make people feel good. Therapists harness that power, and use it to enrich the lives of people who are physically handicapped or who are trapped by mental illness. Performing expressive body movements can give people of all abilities a sense of great freedom and release.

BALLROOM DANCE ON THE BIG SCREEN
Cinema-goers were introduced to the seductive world of Latin ballroom dancing with *Tango* (1998). The movie follows an Argentinian film director, Mario Suarez (played by Miguel Ángel Solá), who wants to make the best-ever tango film. In the process, Suarez falls in love with a beautiful, talented young dancer, Elena (played by Mía Maestro).

NEW BALLETS
While many ballet performances are old classics, there are new ballets being written that you could look out for, too. *The Sandpaper Ballet* was first performed by the San Francisco Ballet in 1999. It was set to music by the American composer Leroy Anderson, and one of the pieces sounds just like someone scratching sandpaper.

SYLVIE GUILLEM

Every generation of dancers has its stars, and it is well worth trying to see them perform. French prima ballerina Sylvie Guillem is one. In 2000 she danced as Marguerite in Frederick Ashton's *Marguerite and Armand*, a part originally written for Margot Fonteyn. Guillem is the first ballerina that the Ashton Estate has allowed to perform the dance.

Together, the arms form an extended line

PARIS OPERA OPULENCE

If you are lucky enough to be in Paris, France, visit the Opéra de Paris Garnier. The building itself is a work of art with its sculptures and friezes. However, to the dance enthusiast, it is most interesting as the home of the world's oldest ballet company, founded by Jean-Baptiste Lully in 1672. Nearby, the Musée de l'Opéra has a collection of memorabilia, which includes ballet slippers that belonged to Vaslav Nijinsky.

Guillem dances en pointe

A GLIMPSE BACKSTAGE

Many venues, including London's Royal Opera House, UK, above, allow visitors to sneak behind the scenes when there are no performances. Tourists can see how the lighting rigs work, and where the orchestra sits. They can also see where all the costumes are stored, and look at the dancers' dressing rooms.

Places to visit

THE BRITISH MUSEUM, LONDON, UK
A museum with vast collections of artefacts from around the world, including dance costumes and masks, and featuring:
• An embroidered silk costume worn by a Tibetan monk for a masked dance
• Wooden masks worn by Yoruba dancers in Nigeria

MUSÉE DE L'OPÉRA, PARIS, FRANCE
This museum houses a collection of ballet artefacts, including:
• Ballet slippers that belonged to the ballet dancer, Vaslav Nijinsky
• Playbills, programmes, and set designs for ballets performed at the Paris Opera House

METROPOLITAN MUSEUM OF ART, NEW YORK, USA
A huge museum with cultural exhibits from around the world. Highlights include:
• Masks, costumes, and musical instruments from Africa, Oceania, and the Americas
• A unique costume collection, which has dance outfits and examples of traditional folk dress

THE THEATRE MUSEUM, LONDON, UK
Dedicated to the performing arts, this museum has memorabilia related to plays, ballets, and musicals. Its attractions include:
• Diaghilev-designed costumes and sets from the Ballets Russes
• Comprehensive archive of live ballet recordings

THE HARD NUT

One of the most exciting things about going to see live performances is discovering how different choreographers interpret classic works – or even how stories can be adapted to different forms of dance. In Brussels, Belgium, in 1991, the Mark Morris Dance Group premiered *The Hard Nut* – an exciting new version of a favourite Tchaikovsky ballet, *The Nutcracker*.

Glossary

ACCOMPANIMENT Music played to complement a dance and add drama.

ARABESQUE In ballet, the movement where a dancer extends one leg back and one arm forward.

BALLET A theatrical dance that tells a story to music.

BALLROOM DANCING Dancing in couples – either at social gatherings or in competitions. Dances performed include the fox-trot, waltz, cha-cha, and tango.

BARRE The handrail that dancers hold when they practise in a dance school.

A can can dancer, painted by Henri de Toulouse-Lautrec

BEDOYO A Javanese court dance performed by women.

BHARATA NATYAM A Hindu temple dance that originated in Madras, southeastern India. Dancers use hand gestures and facial expressions to interpret classical poems about the gods.

BUFFALO DANCE A ritual dance performed by Native Americans to give thanks to the gods for the buffalo.

BUGAKU Japanese court dances accompanied by court music (gagaku), where dancers often wear elaborate masks.

Dervish

BUTOH An experimental modern Japanese dance.

CAKEWALK A ballroom dance dating from 1900, where dancers high-stepped and strutted in a square formation.

CAN CAN Performance dance popular in Paris, France, in the 1800s. Lines of dancing girls lifted their multi-layered petticoats as they high-kicked in time to the music.

CHA-CHA A fast ballroom dance based on the Cuban mambo and popular in the 1950s. The steps are one, two, three, shuffle.

CHARLESTON Dance of the 1920s, involving steps and inverted kicks.

CHINESE OPERA Known in China as *ching-hsi*. A musical theatre form, where the performers sing stories in Mandarin and make stylized movements.

CHOREOGRAPHER Someone who invents sequences of dance moves, usually to music.

CONGA An Afro-Cuban chain dance. The steps are one, two, three, kick.

CORPS DE BALLET The dancers in a ballet who perform together in a unified pattern, in contrast to the soloists.

COSSACK A Russian soldier, famed for competitive, high-kicking dancing.

CUECA A Cuban folk dance performed by couples and accompanied by handclaps.

CZARDAS Hungary's national dance, which starts slowly, then continues into a fast section where couples whirl and snap their heels.

Square dancing

Flamenco dancer's costume

DEMI-POINTE In ballet, standing or dancing on the ball of the foot only.

DERVISH A Sufi Muslim monk who whirls and chants in order to reach a trance-like state that brings him closer to God.

DEVADASI An Indian temple dancer who performs the bharata natyam. The word means "handmaiden of god".

DOMBA A ritual chain dance practised by young Venda women in South Africa.

DRAGON DANCE Street dance performed by the Chinese, traditionally at New Year, to frighten away evil spirits.

EN POINTE In ballet, standing on the tip of the toes.

ENTRECHAT A jump in which the dancer crosses the feet in the air in a ballet performance.

FLAMENCO A sensual Spanish gypsy dance performed to castanets and guitar music.

FOLK DANCE Any traditional country dance.

FOX-TROT A ballroom dance popular in the 1910s.

GALLIARD A lively European dance for couples, popular in the 1500s and 1600s.

GHOST DANCE A dance performed by Native American Plains Indians to appeal to the gods to bring back the buffalo.

HAKA A Maori war dance.

HIGHLAND DANCE Energetic group dancing from the Scottish Highlands.

HULA A sacred Hawaiian dance, where the women rock their hips back and forth.

Morris dancers

IMPROVIZATION To spontaneously make up a dance, using no planned moves.

IRISH DANCE Folk dancing from Ireland, where the dancer holds their face and torso still, while moving their legs and feet fast.

JAZZ DANCE A rhythmic, improvized dance to jazz music.

KABUKI A traditional Japanese dance-drama performed by men.

KATHAK An energetic classical dance from northern India performed by both men and women, sometimes in pairs. The fast dances are interspersed with sections of mime.

KATHAKALI A classical dance-drama from Kerala, southern India, usually performed by men and boys. Dancers mime to a sung story from a Hindu epic, such as the *Ramayana* or the *Mahabharata*.

A stage musical in Florida

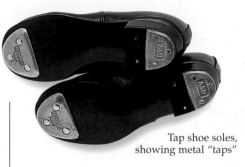

Tap shoe soles, showing metal "taps"

LIMBO A competitive West Indian dance. Dancers bend backwards and shimmy under a low bar.

LINDY HOP A fast, improvized 1930s dance.

LINE DANCE A country dance, where people in lines perform steps in unison, often shouted out by a "caller".

MAZURKA A Polish circle dance performed to bagpipe music, with lots of foot-stamping and heel-clicking.

MORRIS DANCE A traditional English folk dance performed in groups.

MUSICAL A popular western form of theatre, incorporating songs and dance.

NOH A Japanese form of dance-drama that is slow-moving and very powerful.

ORISSI An ancient Indian temple dance from Orissa, eastern India.

PAS DE DEUX In ballet, a dance for two performers, generally a man and a woman.

PLIÉ In ballet, bending the knees while keeping the body upright.

QUETZAL DANCE An Aztec dance performed to honour the supreme god, Quetzalcoatl.

RELEVÉ In ballet, the term for moving the body upwards (a strong rise).

RHYTHM A dancer's timing system, based on a pattern of movement or sound.

SAMBA A fast-moving Brazilian dance.

SCORE Document in which dance steps, or musical notes, are written down.

SQUARE DANCE A folk dance for groups of four couples, with the movements sung out by a "caller".

SYMPHONY A piece of music, usually in several contrasting sections. A symphony is written for the whole orchestra – strings, woodwind, brass, and percussion.

TANGO A passionate ballroom dance from Argentina. Couples take long steps and dramatic pauses.

TAP DANCE Dance performed in tap shoes, which have a piece of metal attached to the sole and heel.

TARANTELLA A flirtatious Italian folk dance performed by couples.

TURKEY TROT An American ballroom dance popular in the 1910s. Couples imitated a turkey's walk, bobbing up and down.

TUTU A frilled skirt worn by ballerinas. The Romantic tutu is calf-length, while the classical tutu reveals all of the dancer's legs.

TWIST A dance popular in the 1960s, performed alone by shaking and shimmying the hips.

VARIATION In ballet, a solo dance.

WALTZ A whirling ballroom dance popular in the 1800s (its name comes from the German word meaning "to spin"). The basic pattern is step, slide, step.

Performing the waltz

67

Eyewitness titles in this series:

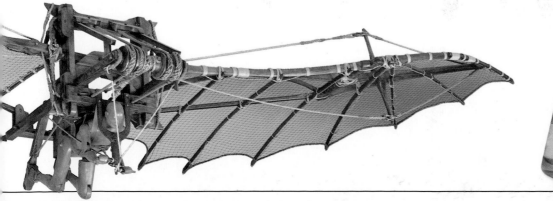

Index

Acknowledgments

Dorling Kindersley would like to thank:
Mary Shanley; Kalamandalam Vijayakumar
at Kala Chethena Kathakali Troupe; Graham Mitchell and the Adonais Ballet Company; Indonesian Embassy and Gillian Roberts; Freed of London Ltd., for supply of ballet shoes; Anusha Subramanyam and Vipul Sangoi; Eric Pierrat at Gallimard Editions.

Editorial and research assistance: Joanne Matthews, Katie Martin, Robert Graham

Design assistance: Goldy Broad, Maggie Tingle, Venice Shone, Elizabeth Nicola.

Additional photography: Susanna Price, Gary Ombler.